THE South African

COOKBOOK

LEOZETTE ROODE

CONTENTS

WELCOME

Welcome to *The South African Vegan Cookbook*. That you've picked up this book and started reading the introduction, brings joy to my healthy, happy, plant-based heart.

BEFORE YOU EMBARK ON THIS JOURNEY

THIS BOOK IS A GUIDE FOR

- curious omnivores wanting to incorporate more plant-based dishes into their diet;
- pescatarians and vegetarians hoping to smoothly transition to a vegan lifestyle;
- cooks, chefs and caterers looking to incorporate more vegan items into their menus;
- new vegans in search of recipes to make at home; and
- experienced vegans longing for simplified, plant-based versions of their family favourites.

I've had many questions about veganism and how best to convert to a plant-based lifestyle. The most honest answer I can give is to simply embark on this journey with great food as your guide — seasoned with a bit of know-how. *The South African Vegan Cookbook* is about down-to-earth food. It features 100 quick, inexpensive and easy-to-follow vegan recipes for the everyday South African. Each delicious dish holds a special place in my heart, and a unique story has inspired many a recipe. Some recipes were also contributed by industry leaders who have shaped my vegan journey.

I keep my kitchen simple and most of my recipes use local ingredients available at a retailer just down the road.

I encourage you to have fun with your food and experiment with the recipes as much as possible — everyone's palate and pantry are different, after all, so substitute the ingredients as you see fit.

MY VEGAN JOURNEY

This might be an everyday book, but it is not every day that an Afrikaans girl with a love for springbok fillet goes vegan.

Growing up in a home where braais were a staple and — to paraphrase the Radio Kalahari Orkes song — chicken was a vegetable, saying no to meat was considered a punishable offence.

I've always tried to be conscious of what I eat, but my first vegan experience unfolded while completing my honours degree in public relations at the Cape Peninsula University of Technology.

For media studies, I was required to try something new and write an article about the experience. I chose to go vegan for one week and I titled my assignment 'Is There Egg in There?'

This was a once-off, so I went back to my meat-eating ways, but continued to tuck into more plant-based meals for health reasons. Then, in June 2012, I saw the graphic animal-rights documentary *Earthlings*.

The reality of the factory-farming industry traumatised me. Tears in my eyes, I immediately decided to transform into a full-time pescatarian: eating fish, eggs and dairy, but no meat.

Eighteen months later, the Veganuary charity challenge popped up on my social media newsfeed. This campaign had inspired me before, so I hopped onboard again: to support veganism, I'd eat a plant-based diet for the entire month of January. During this time, I explored my culinary creativity and physically felt the health benefits of eating green.

I converted permanently.

I was the only vegan I knew and at first I struggled to find restaurants to eat at, ingredients to cook with and friends to confide in, so I created my own platform — the CTVeganista blog.

Initial scribbles of thoughts and recipes quickly transformed into a lifestyle guide for aspiring vegans struggling to find their fix in the Mother City. CTVeganista featured regular posts on plant-based recipes, veg-friendly restaurants, travelling, vegan events and cruelty-free beauty products.

Through my blogging and my determination to make a difference to the lives of farm animals, I began working as campaign manager at Humane Society International, one of the world's biggest animal-protection organisations. I organise welfare campaigns to improve living conditions for South African farm animals; and managed Green Monday SA — a movement encouraging South Africans to 'eat green' on the first day of each week, improving their health, reducing their carbon footprint and helping save animals' lives.

National chain restaurants, celebrities, educational institutions, people from all corners of society and even the Western Cape Government's Department of Health have joined this movement.

Sharing insights on animal welfare and plant-based eating, I have been fortunate to feature in many publications, hosting plant-based cooking demonstrations on national television and conducting talks about veganism at public events and on local radio stations.

The next step in my vegilicious life?

Publishing this cookbook — and hopefully creating a whole lot of positive change.

VEGAN 101

Veganism is a growing phenomenon on the global culinary scene. Every year thousands of people worldwide take the leap, replacing meat, eggs and dairy with plant-based foods such as nuts, grains, beans, legumes and vegetables.

Veganism in South Africa is a relatively new concept and, yes, the movement is expanding. Still, it's rather misunderstood — even frowned upon.

Before understanding the reason to live this way, it might be helpful to know the difference between the common diet types:

OMNIVORE: Is happy to consume animal products, including, but not limited to, meat, fish and dairy, and also plant-based options.

PESCATARIAN: Consumes fish or other seafood, eggs, dairy and plant-based foods, but eliminates all other meat products.

VEGETARIAN: Consumes eggs, dairy and plant-based foods, but eschews all meat products, including fish.

STRICTLY VEGETARIAN / VEGAN / PLANT-BASED / GREEN: Consumes only plant-based foods, including fruit, vegetables, legumes, nuts and grains; eliminates all products derived from animals, including meat, fish, eggs, dairy and honey.

RAW VEGAN: Consumes only uncooked, plant-based foods, or foods cooked at no more than approximately 45°C.

NOTE: A vegan lifestyle is different to a plant-based diet. Although food consumption is identical — purely plant-based — vegans try as far as possible to eliminate animal-derived products and activities from all aspects of their lives.

Vegans try not to use household or personal-care products containing animal derivatives or animal-tested products; wear or use animal-based materials such as leather, wool, fur and silk; and don't take part in activities that use animals for entertainment and entrepreneurship.

A plant-based diet might seem limiting at first, but the reality is that vegans have fantastic food options at their disposal. Many people are surprised how they are able to replace their favourite non-vegan foods and satisfy their cravings with plant-based dishes — like the ones featured in *The South African Vegan Cookbook*.

Every day more plant-based alternatives to meat, dairy and egg products emerge in the market, making it easy to veganise almost any meal.

WHY VEGAN?

Did you know? In South Africa, we raise more than one billion land animals for food every year. Research reveals that these numbers are growing. According to a study in 2013 by Meissner, Scholtz and Palmer in the *South African Journal of Animal Science*, over the past ten years South Africans' pork intake increased by 77%, our poultry consumption by 63%, beef increased by 39%, eggs by 16% and dairy by 11%. All of this comes at a price: the culture of raising animals for food and consuming a diet rich in animal products is destroying our environment and our health.

VEGAN FOR THE ENVIRONMENT

Animal agriculture precipitates climate change, deforestation, water pollution and water shortages. Natural disasters are increasing globally. Specifically here in drought-challenged South Africa, there has never been a more powerful ecological argument to go vegan.

1 WATER RESOURCES: Producing animal-based products requires enormous amounts of water. Did you know that over 4 000 litres of water are needed to produce a single kilogram of chicken meat? Mekonnen and Hoekstra's 2012 study *A global assessment of the water footprint of farm animal products* reports that it takes over 1 000% more water to produce beef compared to wheat. We use water in every stage of factory farming: growing animal feed, hydrating farm animals, disposing of their waste, washing their housing, sanitising slaughtering equipment, and cleaning these products before packaging. Consider this: one of the easiest ways you can reduce your water footprint is by eating more plant-based meals — even if it is just one day a week.

2 WATER POLLUTION: Animal faeces, produced by our factory-farmed animals, plus the chemicals used to grow animal feed, are dumped into our freshwater supply, polluting some of the water that we are so desperately trying to save right now.

3 CLIMATE CHANGE: Greenhouse gases, especially carbon dioxide, methane and nitrous oxide, are released into our atmosphere when we raise animals for food. The gases increase the atmospheric temperature, leading to droughts, wildfires, floods and other climate-related disasters. According to a study conducted in 2013 by the Food and Agriculture Organization of the United Nations (FAO), farm animal production alone accounts for 14,5% of the world's greenhouse gas emissions.

4 LAND: Amazingly, we use more than half of the land in South Africa to raise farm animals for consumption. Grazing animals spoil the land for the many other plant and animal species that live there naturally. A large amount of land is dedicated to growing crops to feed animals – if we use this land to grow crops to feed humans, we could feed significantly more people.

VEGAN FOR HEALTH

Literature increasingly indicates that by reducing the amount of animal-based products we consume, we can improve our health. There are many studies and articles to read online, but be sure to refer only to reliable sources, such as peer-reviewed journals or sites that reference these, such as Nutritionfacts.org. It can be helpful to consult a qualified, plant-based dietician for professional advice on your health.

Here are some significant health benefits obtained from eating plant-based food:

1 OBESITY: The Medical Research Council (MRC) says nearly 30% of men and 56% of women in South Africa are either overweight or obese. Globally there are now more overweight than underweight people. Meat and other animal-derived products are often heavy in cholesterol and saturated fats. However, plant-based food generally contains less or no unsaturated fat, but rather healthier, unsaturated fat. Studies show that people who eat fewer animal products and more plant-based foods have lower rates of obesity.

2 CHRONIC DISEASES: Many diseases with the highest death rates can be prevented, treated and even reversed through a vegan diet. This includes heart disease (the number one killer in the western world), some forms of cancer, type II diabetes and high blood pressure — the world's top fatal health-risk factors. Reducing your meat and dairy intake and eating more grains, beans, vegetables and fruit can significantly lower your risk of dying from these deadly diseases.

■ In 2015, the World Health Organisation shocked the world when it announced that processed meats (hot dogs, polonies and bacon) could cause cancer. It now recommends that people eat more fruits, vegetables, nuts and whole grains; and transition away from saturated animal fats to unsaturated vegetable-oil fats.

3 CONSTIPATION AND COLON DISEASE: According to the *South African Medical Journal*, colon cancer is the fourth most common cancer in South Africa. This might be linked to a lack of fibre; studies show that the number of hours it takes for your food to travel through your digestive system could determine your risk of getting this disease. Fibre helps the body to digest food quickly. Plant-based foods, such as vegetables, fruits, nuts, beans and grains, are high in fibre. Animal-based products, such as eggs, beef or chicken, provide no fibre.

4 HEALTHY SKIN: A radiant exterior starts within. A plant-based diet of fresh fruits and vegetables, nuts, grains and beans rich in vitamins, minerals and antioxidants will help give you a gorgeous glow. Studies show that omitting meat, eggs and dairy from your diet might improve eczema.

5 ATHLETIC PERFORMANCE: Studies reveal that eating vegan can improve your athletic performance. Plant-based foods are anti-inflammatory, rich in antioxidants, vitamins and minerals and, most importantly, chock-full of highly alkalising foods. Animal products build up acidity in the body, making it harder for muscles to recover after an athletic performance. A diet high in fruits and vegetables holds different benefits altogether: nitrate-rich foods, like beetroot and fennel seeds, can augment athletic performance by boosting oxygen delivery and helping maintain your body's oxygen levels at high altitudes. Many international elite athletes are switching to a plant-based diet, including Patrik Baboumian (vegan strongman), Venus Williams (tennis player), Lewis Hamilton (Formula 1 racing driver), Nate Diaz (mixed martial artist), Tony Gonzalez and David Carter (NFL players), Rich Roll (triathlete), Carl Lewis (track athlete), Heather Mills (skier), and Mac Danzig (mixed martial arts star).

VEGAN FOR ANIMALS

Lastly — but most importantly to me — eating vegan helps reduce animal suffering. The fact that farm animals make up the majority of abused animals globally should come as no surprise.

■ According to the Food and Agriculture Organization (FAO)

of the United Nations, approximately 77 billion land animals are raised per year for human consumption globally and in South Africa alone more than one billion animals per year are slaughtered. This excludes fish and other marine life, bird life and insects such as bees and worms.

■ Factory farming is one of the cruellest practices in the world. Whatever farmers might argue, there is no humane way to kill a living being. Many farm animals raised for food in South Africa endure intensive confinement. Due to a lack of available information and transparent communication, South Africans often remain unaware of what goes on behind barn doors.

■ South Africans consume 7.8 billion eggs each year. More than 95% of these are sourced from hens that spend all their lives in battery cages — that is 95% of the 24.3 million hens raised for egg production. A battery cage is a small wire box that provides an egg-laying hen with less space than an A4-size paper. These cages prevent hens from performing any of their natural behaviours — they can't nest, perch, run, jump or even flap their wings. Because of this, the hens suffer from psychological stress, enduring physical pain like bone breakage, feather loss and metabolic disorders.

■ Similar to hens, more than 50% of pregnant sows in South Africa spend their lives in gestation crates. Gestation crates are individual metal stalls that confine pregnant sows in the commercial pork production industry. Here they are unable to exercise, fully extend their legs or even turn around.

■ The dairy industry is as distressing as meat production. Dairy cows produce milk for exactly the same reason we do: to feed their young, so the only way for cows to produce milk — for human consumption — is to fall pregnant. In factory farms cows are inseminated at a young age. The calf is removed from its mother so that the farmers can collect milk for human consumption. Studies show that both mom and baby suffer psychological stress following this separation. The dairy cow lactates for a few months, after which, she is inseminated again to repeat the process. Once a cow's milk production starts to decrease, she gets slaughtered.

■ Farm animals, much like domesticated animals, including cats, dogs and rabbits, have personalities. By eating more plant-based foods, we can decrease the demand for animal products and, ultimately reduce the number of sentient beings that have to be harmed for human food consumption.

I AM A VEGAN. WHAT NOW?

When transitioning to a plant-based lifestyle, empower yourself with as much knowledge as possible. If you're clued up on how to embrace this inspiring new cuisine and way of living, you'll be armed with a powerful education as the questions start rolling in.

There are hundreds of books on vegan nutrition, as well as documentaries on veganism and animal welfare. Online reviews abound on the latest products, vegan-friendly restaurants and up-and-coming events.

Join a vegan community for support and guidance along the way — this is fun and can be very helpful.

Important websites
■ Beauty Without Cruelty: bwcsa.co.za
■ Cape Town Vegan: capetownvegan.com
■ CTVeganista: ctveganista.com
■ Green Monday SA: greenmonday.co.za
■ Happy Cow: www.happycow.net
■ Humane Society International: www.hsi.org
■ Nutritionfacts.org: nutritionfacts.org
■ Proveg International: proveg.com
■ SA Vegan Society: vegansociety.org.za
■ The Green Dietitian: thegreendietitian.co.za
■ Vegan SA: www.vegansa.com
■ Veganuary: veganuary.com
■ Vegilicious: vegilicious.co.za

Facebook groups and pages
■ Boere Vegans
■ Cape Town Vegan Challenge
■ Stellenbosch Vegans and Vegetarians
■ Vegan Good News
■ Vegan Parenting in South Africa
■ Vegan Society South Africa

COMMON VEGAN QUESTIONS ANSWERED

What about protein?

After being asked what vegans actually eat, the next most common question is where I get my protein from. There is a big misconception that plant-based foods cannot provide you with enough protein. However, healthcare professionals have thoroughly busted this myth. Eating an array of plant foods gives us all the protein our bodies need — but the emphasis here is on diversity.

Protein-packed, plant-based foods include tofu, beans, chickpeas, green peas, sprouts, spinach, brown rice, broccoli, hemp, brown bread, lentils, peanut butter, seitan, oats, bulgur wheat, chia seeds, sesame seeds (including tahini), pasta, almonds, nutritional yeast, textured vegetable protein … and the list goes on.

And what about iron?

I struggled with iron deficiency even before I transformed to a vegan lifestyle. Our bodies need iron to keep the oxygen circulating throughout the bloodstream, and a shortage can cause serious illness. Thankfully, plant-based foods — including black beans, kidney beans, lentils, oats, pumpkin seeds, soya products, spinach, chickpeas and even whole-wheat bread — brim with iron. Eat enough of these, complemented by vitamin C for improved iron absorption, and you're not likely to experience problems.

But we need milk for calcium . . .

You know that we need calcium for strong teeth and bones — that fact has been drilled into our memory from a young age. What you might not know is that you can consume all the calcium you need through plants. Plant-based foods often have an even higher calcium content than dairy products. Try to include an assortment of broccoli, beans, dark leafy greens, such as kale and collard greens, nuts, seeds or soya products — and your bones should be just fine.

Can I get all my essential fats through a vegan diet?

Yes, good fats are plentiful in a vegan diet. By eating an assortment of fruits and vegetables, you will absorb all the omega-6 fatty acids your body desires. Omega-3 fatty acids are a bit trickier. To ensure you get enough of this important fatty acid, consider eating chia seeds, flaxseeds, ground flax, flax oil, hempseed oil or walnuts daily and add, or take a daily supplement.

Is eating vegan expensive?

A plant-based diet might as well be the most inexpensive way of eating, if you stick to wholefoods. Grains, beans, seasonal fruits and vegetables are some of the cheapest ingredients on the market, especially when you buy in bulk. Let's not forget: it's meat, egg and dairy products that really break the bank. That said, if you're going to purchase processed and luxurious vegan products, such as superfood powders, truffle oil and organic maple syrup, you're likely to see an uptick or two in your expenses. Also, when dining out the vegetarian and vegan meals are often the most inexpensive options on the menu.

Do you lose weight on a vegan diet?

Another question I get asked often. A diet of plants is as healthy as you can get and, yes, most vegans lose weight when swapping their meat, eggs and dairy for plant-based alternatives. Still, there is no lack of vegan junk food doing the rounds. If you're going to base your plant-food preferences on bread, fries, Oreos, crisps and melted vegan cheese toasties, then you're going to struggle to drop a size. The best foods for maintaining a healthy weight are those that are high in nutrients and low in calories: these are usually the plant-based, wholefood options.

What happens if we stop eating animals?

Cows will not take over the world. As mentioned earlier in the book, almost all cows are artificially inseminated, so they don't breed unless we make them. Animals are farmed according to consumer demands.

When we eat fewer animals, farmers will produce fewer animal products and breed fewer farm animals. The world is not going vegan overnight so we will, hopefully, see a gradual decrease in farm animals.

What would happen to the land we use for factory farming?

Land used for raising animals could be harnessed to raise

crops instead: for starters, to feed our growing human population rather than farm animals. Ultimately, we can end world hunger. Alternatively, farms could always transform into animal sanctuaries — wink.

Isn't too much fruit bad for you?

Doctors and diabetics are often concerned with the amount of sugar in fruits, but new literature shows that low-dose fructose might help our bodies to control blood-sugar levels. Sugars in fruit don't raise sugar levels to the same extent as refined sugar and having a piece of fruit with every dish could help you lower, not raise, your blood sugar.

Do I need to take any supplements?

Omnivores who eat animal-derived products consume vitamin B12 because the bacteria within animals' bodies produce it. Alternatively, vegans should consider vitamin B12 supplements, or take in a lot of vitamin B12-fortified foods, such as soya milk. Even many meat eaters would benefit from additional B12. It might be useful to test your blood on a yearly basis, regardless of your chosen diet, and seek the advice of a medical professional.

Isn't soya unhealthy?

Soya is greatly misunderstood. It is made from soya beans and contains phyto-oestrogens (plant oestrogens), or 'isoflavones'. Phyto-oestrogens are not the same as the oestrogen our bodies produce naturally. So, boys, you won't grow 'man-boobs' from eating soya. High levels of oestrogen can raise the likelihood of developing breast cancer, whereas phyto-oestrogen seems to lower the risk — it is said to have pro-oestrogenic effects on some body tissues and anti-oestrogenic effects on others.

NOTE: Be sure to only consume non-genetically modified soya products.

Can children eat vegan?

A plant-based diet can be the healthiest diet you and your children can follow. It can provide all the essential nutrients they need to grow up as strongly and healthily as possible.

It is key that they eat a good diversity of plant-based foods and healthy quantities too.

You'll be surprised to find that there are plenty of plant-based options that even the fussiest kids will love! I recommend testing lots of different options to see what your kids like most, including roasting veggies and puréeing them into dips, or making veggie patties and pasta bakes. *The South African Vegan Cookbook* packs in many imaginative ideas on how to cook plants!

Can I eat vegan while pregnant?

Provided you consume all the nutrients as well as supplements your body needs, such as vitamin B12, your baby should be healthy too. I have never been as healthy as I'm right now, thriving on my vegan diet. Why would I go back to my meat-eating ways when pregnant?

It is, of course, important to see a healthcare professional when eating for two — vegan or not. Make sure you visit a certified medical professional who will be open-minded about your vegan choices.

In modern living, veganism is still a relatively new concept. Be prepared that your general practitioner, dietician or gynaecologist might advise you against this lifestyle because they are not up-to-date with the latest nutritional research. If this does happen, I would recommend consulting a vegan nutritionist and discussing the doctor's specific concerns.

Why don't vegans eat honey?

Vegans try not to consume products produced by or derived from animals, where possible, and honey is made by bees. Some beekeepers and honey producers follow more ethical practices, but commercial producers might harvest this liquid gold and replace it with sugar syrup. Hardly as nutritious — not forgetting how hard these little critters work in the first place to produce honey for the hive. During the harvesting process, honeybees might become injured, wither and die. Consider watching *Vanishing of the Bees*, a documentary that tracks the disappearance of honeybees across the planet.

How do I know if it's vegan?

Often, especially with products that are not packaged, you'll need to ask someone whether a specific product is vegan, for instance muffins at a café. In stores you can simply look at labels. When you first make the leap to a vegan diet, reading labels will become part of your every shopping spree. Don't be discouraged; you will soon know your plant-based products off by heart. Here are a few label red flags:

- **Beef:** This isn't just meat. It's also present in flavourings.
- **Beeswax:** Obtained from honeycomb and used in confectionary goods; as a coating for cheese, fruits and vegetables; in some bubble gum; and many personal-care products.
- **Butter, butterfat, buttermilk, butter oil:** Found in many food items, including biscuits, chocolates, puddings and baked goods.
- **Casein:** A form of milk protein used to filtrate alcohol. Found in creams, puddings, milk products, powders, creamy soups and more.
- **Cochineal insects:** Red food colouring made from the pulverised insect. Watch out for this in many red food items: drinks, sweets, food colouring, tomato sauce, dairy products, medicine and personal-care products, too.
- **Eggs:** Present in many sauces (especially mayonnaise), confectionary items, batter products and baked goods.
- **Gelatine:** A product produced by boiling skin, cartilage, ligaments and bones (usually cows and pigs). In gummy sweets, jelly, many low-fat foods, margarines, medicine capsules, marshmallows, jams, bubblegum, ice cream, yoghurt and desserts.
- **Ghee:** A clarified butter popular in Asian foods.
- **Glycerine:** Made from animal fat; used as a sweetener and preservative. Common in many personal-care products.
- **Honey:** Often used in sauces and dressing, sweets and energy bars, and bread and other baked goods.
- **Lactose:** A form of milk sugar used in crisps (note those cheesy flavours), sweets and food powders.
- **Milk, milk fat, milk powder, milk solids:** Pervasive in food products — from powders, drinks and chocolates, to wine and crisps.
- **Shellac:** The female lac bug secretes this resin. Employed as a glaze in confectionary goods, fruits and vegetables.
- **Whey:** A protein made from milk, whey is a byproduct of the cheese-manufacturing process. Popular in protein powders, sweets, baked goods, butter, cheese, creams, cereals, crisps and bread.

Is alcohol vegan?

A lot of booze contains animal products, or has been filtered using animal parts and products. Yes, milk is found in some wines and creamy liqueurs and gelatine, egg whites, casein (milk protein) and even fish bladders are used as fining agents for filtering alcoholic beverages. Luckily, that doesn't mean you have to give up your favourite thirst-quencher. Many wines, ciders, beers and hard liquor are vegan. Simply do a bit of research: the Vegan SA website lists a mixture of animal-free brands. Or, opt for distilled spirits such as vodka, gin, whiskey and brandy.

Is palm oil vegan?

Palm oil is a plant-based product that does not contain any animal-derived ingredients, so in essence it should be vegan. However, the global rise of palm-oil plantations has led to rainforest destruction. Many species, specifically orangutans, are often fatally impacted by the loss of their habitat. Vegans don't support any form of animal abuse and, if palm-oil production is killing orangutans, many feel it cannot be considered vegan. Palm oil is mostly present in processed foods, which you can completely avoid on a vegan diet.

Still, this is a debatable topic among vegans the world over. I always sketch this scenario: if my dad is interested in going vegan and I take him shopping, we fill his trolley to the brim with all the vegan alternatives that will make his transitioning journey easier, including meat replacements, biscuits, crisps, pizza bases, sauces, chocolates and pastries. He feels confident that he won't need meat, eggs and dairy as part of his diet.

Now I remove all the products containing palm oil — including his essential meat, dairy and egg replacements — and my dad is left with only fresh fruits, vegetables, grains, beans and a limited number of processed products. Suddenly eating vegan seems extremely difficult.

For a long-time vegan with experience in plant-based cooking, it is much easier to avoid products containing palm oil. Although I don't encourage the consumption and production of palm oil, my dad going vegan using palm-oil products is better than him not going vegan at all.

EQUIPMENT LIST

ESSENTIAL

Blender: My number-one kitchen appliance. A high-speed blender is optimal, but expensive and not essential. If you're not ready to invest in pricey kitchen equipment, a hand blender, Nutribullet or jug blender will work perfectly well.

Food processor: A food processor is different to a blender. It is used for puréeing, chopping, slicing and shredding. Like blenders, it is a kitchen essential.

Sieve: Standard stuff … for sifting dry ingredients; draining and rinsing fine grains and beans.

Strainer: Invest in a strainer for pasta, vegetables, rice and so forth.

Silicone spatula: Great for using in your pots and pans without scraping the surface. Essential for scooping out the last bit of mixture from your food processor and blender. A spoon just doesn't do the trick.

A good set of non-stick pots and pans: An obvious essential, for cooking almost everything in this book. Make sure you have at least one saucepan that can go onto the fire, if you love braaiing like me.

A good set of knives: Another obvious must-have, this time for breezy slicing and chopping. There is nothing as frustrating as ruining a beautifully cooked dish with a blunt cutting knife.

Oven gloves: It is impossible to count how many times I've burnt my fingers, hands and even arms while producing this cookbook!

NOT ESSENTIAL

Spiraliser: Amazing for transforming plant starches, vegetables and fruit into noodles. Homeware stores now stock different price brackets. Otherwise, simply grate the vegetables or cut them into strips using a mandoline slicer.

Juicer: Invest in one of these babies if you want to make freshly squeezed, pulp-free juices. I have one at home, but don't find myself using it as often as I thought I would. The budget option? Grab your blender and strain the mixture through cheesecloth.

Cheesecloth: Cheap, porous material up for grabs at your local material shop. Strain homemade juices, homemade nut or soya milk and homemade nut-based cheese. You're not likely to call on it often, so it is not a necessity.

Dehydrator: Lovely for producing mushroom biltong, kale chips, dried fruits and other raw vegan snacks. Or, use your oven — put it on a low setting and leave the oven door slightly open.

Tofu press: Quite hard to come by in South Africa. It's also quite pricey, but perfect for draining liquid from your tofu. I personally use paper towels and a heavy cookbook.

Veggie chop: A little gadget, like the Twister, that chops your veggies in seconds. Ideal if you're in a rush to whip up a meal, feeling lazy or don't want onion tears to ruin your mascara (I'm the proud owner of one too, so don't feel ashamed).

Pressure cooker: Old-school on the stove top, or the new electrical versions will do. I use mine a lot for cooking up dried grains and beans that usually take hours on the stove.

Air-fryer: Glorious for the health-conscious. Cook almost everything without added oil and still enjoy ultimate crispiness.

MY VEGAN-FRIENDLY KITCHEN ALTERNATIVES

MEAT

- The Fry Family Food Co.'s 25-plus meat alternatives include patties and sausages; chicken-style nuggets, pops and strips; battered prawn-style pieces, pies, curry pieces, mince, hot dogs, pies, sausage rolls, butternut balls and falafels.
- Quorn's range of vegetarian products and four vegan meat alternatives incorporates nuggets, schnitzels, spicy burger patties and savoury pieces. Make sure you only purchase the products that display the 'vegan' ribbon on the cover.
- Denny's Mushrooms recently launched mushroom-based patties, nuggets and pops.
- Urban Vegan produces burger bites, patties, boerewors, standard sausages, bacon, yoghurt and cheese.

DAIRY

- Almond Breeze features these delicious flavours: Original, Unsweetened and Barista Blend (ideal for lattes and cappuccinos).
- Clover's Good Hope soya range features non-GM soya milks, including flavoured ranges.
- Violife offers coconut-oil based vegan cheeses and cheese spreads. Its 'For Pizza' cheese is my favourite meltable cheese.
- Irene's Gourmet includes a selection of cheeses, including vegan Parmesan.
- Utopia Cheese's yoghurts and cashew-nut cheeses are inspiring.
- Nature & Moi is a new French vegan cheese company that brings you the market's most affordable vegan-cheese products in three ranges: Cheddar, mozzarella and Gouda.
- Le-Coquin produces coconut yoghurt and delicious Cheddar cheese and vegan soft serve.
- Consider the many other vegan cheese, milk, yoghurt and ice-cream products on the international market: although local, of course, comes first.

- For a great non-dairy cream, use one of Orley Whip's two varieties.
- A spare can of coconut milk and coconut cream should always be in your pantry.

JELLY

- Simply Delish jelly is sugar-free, fat-free and gelatine-free.

MARGARINE

- Olé maragrine is nice to vegans and available at most retailers. If unsure which margarine to use, consult you local vegan community.

PASTA

Most store-bought, dried pastas don't include egg. Still, always read the label to make sure.
- Happy Earth People's two pulse pastas (chickpea pasta and red-lentil pasta) are packed with protein and are gluten-free.

WINE

I've listed my favourite vegan wines below. For more options, refer to the Vegan SA website.
NOTE: Some wine farms have only certain vegan cultivars. Before you make a purchase, do your research or give them a quick call.
- Stellar Organics
- Delheim
- Durbanville Hills
- Leopard's Leap
- Vondeling
- Boschkloof Wines
- Douglas Green
- D'Aria
- Elgin Ridge
- Fairview Wines
- Glen Carlou
- Haute Cabrière

- Graham Beck
- Lothian Vineyards
- Longridge
- Org de Rac (they have the best Chardonnay — just saying)
- Spice Route Wines
- Vrede & Lust
- Warwick Wine Estate

BISCUITS

- Oreos. Yes. Oreos.
- Baumann's Marie Biscuits.
- Bakers Biscuits incorporates four vegan ranges: Ginger Nuts, Romany Tarte, Digestives and Snacktime party-pack biscuits.
- Pick n Pay, Spar and Woolworths offer vegan biscuits and crackers under their house brands. Just double-check the labels.
- Ouma Rusks' muesli and condensed-milk flavours are vegan.
- The Allergen Baker flogs vegan rusks, crunchies and biscuits.

MAYONNAISE

- B-Well sells four egg-free, vegan mayonnaises: The Creamy Gourmet (my favourite), The Original Tangy, The Reduced Oil and The Olive & Canola.
- Crosse & Blackwell Trim Original and Trim 1 000 Island Sauce are both vegan.
- That Mayo has two vegan mayonnaise varieties.

EGGS

- Orgran 'No-Egg' powder is an egg replacer I recommend for baking. It is available in most food and health stores.
- Flax egg: Mix one tablespoon of ground flaxseed (buy it in a powder) with three tablespoons water to create one egg substitute. (Let the mixture thicken for five minutes before using it.)
- Aquafaba (canned chickpea brine) can be used instead of eggs. Whipped up, it makes perfect meringues.
- Applesauce and mashed bananas can serve as egg substitutes in baking.
- Tofu — another *eggcellent* substitute, especially for recipes that need a lot of eggs, like quiches. Puree a ¼ cup silken tofu to create an egg substitute.

CHOCOLATE

- Most dark chocolates are dairy free, but always read the labels to be sure. Some of my favourites are: Lindt, Beacon, Honest Chocolate, De Villiers Chocolate, Zang and Aero.
- Beacon Midnight Velvet Chocolate is my go-to vegan chocolate for baking. Its Niki dark chocolate / coconut slab is vegan.
- Honest Chocolate's chocolate slabs, desserts, spreads and truffles are a vegan's delight.
- ZANG caffeinated dark chocolate is great for when you need a pick-me-up.
- Beacon's dark chocolate TV bar is a vegan bonbon — but not the small chocolate bar.
- Aero's dark chocolate slab contains no animal products.

OTHER BRANDS AND PRODUCTS

- Ina Paarman brings us her famous herbs and spices, pestos, sauces and spreads. Not all products are vegan, so read the labels carefully.
- Pesto Princess stocks dairy-free pestos as well as a hummus.
- Health Connection Wholefoods and Nature's Choice make hundreds of vegan-smart health products. The following are in my daily staple: A deactivated yeast that comes in the form of flakes, nutritional yeast has a strong cheesy, nutty flavour and we use it to make sauce. Superb on kale chips, salads and sandwiches; and it's super-healthy. Bag it in the health aisle of local retailers or at health stores.
- Tahini is a sesame-seed paste, made by blending roasted sesame seeds. Essential in hummus and used in many smoothies, sauces and curries. You can purchase it at your local retailer, but it is much cheaper to buy in bulk at Eastern groceries. I usually buy a 1 kg tub at Atlas Trading Company in Cape Town..

STOCK UP

Eating vegan is easy when you have filled your pantry and fridge with the vegan-friendly food essentials. Most supermarkets now stock the basics, such as non-dairy milk, vegan margarine, meat alternatives, oils, flours and condiments. If you can't find what you need at your local retailer, order online from websites like Wellness Warehouse, Faithful to Nature, Fresh Earth Food Store and Pink Piggy Lifestyle.

This comprehensive list is designed as a loose, practical guide on what to buy, so don't feel overwhelmed by the number of food items I've mentioned. You definitely don't need all of them. Shop smartly to build up your stocks gradually and economically.

The first step is to replace your everyday ingredients with vegan alternatives. After doing so you can spoil yourself with different powders, spices and sauces. At first, it is important to read labels carefully, but soon you will have memorised an ample inventory to make vegan-food shopping a breeze. Do your research and shop around for products that are available in bulk, or even better, grow and make your own.

IN YOUR FRIDGE

- **Fresh tofu:** Marinated, silken, firm and extra-firm tofu. Available from Chinese supermarkets, Spar, Woolworths and health shops such as Wellness Warehouse.
- **A collection of fresh fruits and vegetables:** Always try to buy seasonal fruits and vegetables, the more environmentally friendly option.
- **Vegan cheese:** Coconut oil or cashew nut-based cheeses and cheese spreads. Available from Woolworths, Spar, Shoprite Checkers, Pick n Pay, Wellness Warehouse and other health stores.
- **Vegan butter or margarine:** Available from most local retailers and health stores.
- **Tahini:** Sesame paste. Available from local retailers, health shops, online stores and in bulk from Eastern grocers.
- **Vegan yoghurt:** Soya or nut-based. Available from selected retailers, such as Woolworths and Spar, health shops, markets and online stores.
- **Vegan wine:** See my vegan wine suggestions on page 14.
- **Fruit or vegetable juice**
- **Hummus and vegan pestos**
- **A selection of fresh herbs:** basil, rosemary, mint, chives, spring onion, sage, coriander, parsley, thyme, dill and many more.

IN YOUR FREEZER

- **Multiple meat alternatives,** including soya mince, sausages, patties, nuggets, strips, pies, pops, hot dogs and schnitzels.
- **Frozen fruits,** such as berries, mangos and bananas.
- **Frozen vegetables,** including stir-fry, cruciferous (cauliflower, cabbage, Brussels sprouts and so on), spinach and peas.
- Puff pastry and phyllo pastry.
- Vegan ice cream
- Wraps and rotis
- A few portions of cooked grains

IN YOUR PANTRY

- **Canned foods**
  Chickpeas
  Baked beans
  Butter beans
  Black beans
  Mixed vegetables
  Lentils
  Coconut milk
  Coconut cream
  Sweetcorn
  Tomato and onion mix

- **Non-dairy milk**
  Almond milk
  Unsweetened soya milk
  Rice milk

- **Dried legumes**
  Lentils: red, brown, split
  Chickpeas
  Assorted beans: black beans, soya beans or soya chunks, kidney beans, sugar beans and so on
  Chickpea flour

- **Grains**
  Rice: brown rice, white rice, sushi rice
  Buckwheat
  Pasta
  Flour: all purpose, bread flour, cake-wheat flour
  Couscous
  Quinoa

Millet
Barley
Samp
Mealiemeal
Oats
Cereals
Polenta

■ Nuts, seeds and dried fruits

These might be an expensive luxury, but you can buy them on special to keep more coins in your pocket. It is important to remember that nuts and seeds are a necessary part of your diet, but you need to consume them only in small quantities.

Chia seeds
Flaxseeds
Raw cashews
Raw almonds
Pine nuts
Sunflower seeds
Sesame seeds
Dates
Cranberries
Goji berries
Pumpkin seeds

■ Oils and fats

One or more of the following oils:
Olive oil
Coconut oil
Sunflower oil
Sesame-seed oil
Avocado oil
Macadamia oil

■ Treats Many treats, sweets, crisps and chips are, in fact, vegan. However, always read the label and look out for ingredients such as cow's milk, whey powder and gelatine. Stock up on treats and savoury snacks, too, so that you won't feel like you're missing out.

Biscuits (see page 15)
Rusks (see page 15)
Crisps
Dark chocolate (see page 15)

■ Dried herbs and spices

I love experimenting with different flavours, therefore I keep a long list of herbs and spices but they are too many to mention. This list includes the spices I use almost daily, and has a prominent feature in *The South African Vegan Cookbook*. Always keep your spices in an airtight container to seal in the flavour. Buy whole spices instead of powdered ones — the former keeps its flavour longer. Shopping in bulk from Eastern grocers like Atlas Trading in Cape Town will net you quality, economical products.

Turmeric
Cumin
Coriander
Cinnamon
Nutmeg
Cayenne pepper
Paprika
Onion powder
Mustard powder
Curry powder
Vegetable stock powder
Mixed Herbs
Origanum
Rosemary
Thyme

Salt
Black pepper
Kala namak (Indian black salt that tastes just like boiled eggs, available from Woolworths, Eastern grocers, online retailers and health shops)
Nutritional yeast

■ Condiments, spreads, sauces and liquids

Egg-free mayonnaise, available from most local retailers
Tomato sauce
Apple-cider vinegar
Balsamic vinegar
Lemon juice
Sweet-chilli sauce
Hot sauce: Tabasco and Sriracha
Mustard: English mustard, Dijon mustard, wholegrain mustard
Soya sauce
Maple syrup
Peanut butter
Marmite
Agave syrup
Stevia
Vanilla essence
Tomato paste
Passata (sieved tomato mixture)

■ Other

Orgran egg replacer
Baking powder
Bicarbonate of soda
White onion soup
Brown onion soup
Olives

It's early in the morning

Beet & Berry-Bliss Smoothie

INGREDIENTS

2 cups almond milk

2 frozen bananas

1 cup strawberries (about 6)

1 cup frozen blueberries

3 to 5 dates, pitted

1 tablespoon flaxseed powder

1 small beet, peeled and chopped

INSTRUCTIONS

1. Blend all the ingredients in a blender or food processor until smooth. Transfer to glasses and enjoy.

Serves 1 to 2 | Under 30 minutes

Omega-3 Blueberry Smoothie

INGREDIENTS

½ cup flaxseeds

½ cup walnuts

½ cup tofu

2 cups frozen berries

3 tablespoons agave nectar

2 cups almond milk

INSTRUCTIONS

1. Add the flaxseeds and walnuts to a blender. Blend until they form a very fine powder. Add the tofu, berries, agave and almond milk to the blender. Blend until you've combined all the ingredients. Top with frozen berries and serve immediately.

Healthy Chocolate Granola

INGREDIENTS

3 cups (330 g) oats
½ cup sunflower seeds
½ cup mixed nuts
¼ cup shredded coconut
1 teaspoon ground cinnamon
3 large, ripe bananas
10 pitted dried dates, soaked in boiling water
3 heaped tablespoons raw cacao
¼ cup water
½ cup cacao nibs / chopped dark chocolate (optional)

INSTRUCTIONS

1. Preheat the oven to 150°C. Line a baking tray with baking paper, glossy side down. Mix all the dry ingredients in a big mixing bowl (excluding the cacao nibs / chopped chocolate).
2. Blend the bananas, dates, cacao and water in a high-speed blender. Add the chocolate sauce to the dry ingredients and mix through until everything is coated.
3. Scoop the mixture onto the lined baking tray and use a spatula to spread and evenly flatten out the mixture. Place in the oven for 25 minutes (make sure you don't burn the nuts).
4. Remove from the heat and let the mixture cool. When cold and hard, crumble into pieces. If it is not crunchy enough, place the mixture back into the oven for another 5 to 10 minutes.
5. Add the cacao nibs or chopped chocolate and place in an airtight container.

Choc-nut Quinoa Breakfast Bowl

INGREDIENTS

½ cup white quinoa

1 cup water

Pinch of salt

½ cup to 1 cup almond milk

1 tablespoon cocoa powder

2 tablespoons peanut butter powder

1 tablespoon maple syrup (or another sweetener
of your choice)

Toppings

Choc chips, peanut butter, cacao nibs,
coconut flakes, nuts

INSTRUCTIONS

1. Rinse the quinoa until the water runs clear.
2. Place the quinoa in a pot with the cup water and the pinch of salt. Bring to the boil.
3. As soon as it's bubbling, lower the heat and simmer the quinoa for 15 minutes, with the lid on.
4. Remove the lid, add the almond milk, cocoa, peanut butter powder and maple syrup and stir through. Let it cook for 5 minutes.
5. Transfer the quinoa porridge to your breakfast bowl, add your toppings, some more peanut butter, and more almond milk if you desire.

Go-to Chocolate Peanut Butter & Coffee Smoothie

INGREDIENTS

½ cup rolled oats

1 cup silken tofu

1 cup almond milk

½ cup water

¼ cup almonds

6 dried dates

2 tablespoons raw cacao

1 tablespoon flaxseeds

1 tablespoon chia seeds

1 tablespoon peanut butter

1 teaspoon ground coffee (you can use decaf)

Toppings

Cacao nibs, chocolate granola, peanut putter

INSTRUCTIONS

1. Add all the ingredients to a blender and blend until smooth.
2. Pour into glasses, scatter with cacao nibs, chocolate granola and another helping of peanut butter.

Double-thick Choc-mint Smoothie

INGREDIENTS

1¼ cups almond milk

2 bananas

1 cup silken tofu

6 to 8 dates, pitted

2 tablespoons cacao

1 tablespoon peanut butter

1 tablespoon cacao nibs

2 tablespoons flaxseed powder

2 drops peppermint oil

4 leaves fresh mint / 1 drop peppermint oil / a few drops Flavour Nation choc-mint essence

INSTRUCTIONS

1. Blend all the ingredients in a blender or food processor and chill in the fridge.
2. Line the inside of some glasses with chocolate syrup or chocolate nut butter. Add the smoothie mix to the glasses.
3. Top with more cacao nibs and fresh mint.

Creamy Banana Oats Smoothie

This smoothie might not be fruity, but it is still a healthy treat. Amend the banana according to your taste buds. For an extra kick, add a vegan vanilla protein powder.

INGREDIENTS

2 cups almond milk
2 to 3 frozen bananas
2 tablespoons roasted macadamia butter / almond butter
2 tablespoons coconut sugar
1 teaspoon ground cinnamon
½ cup rolled oats
1 teaspoon vanilla essence
1 tablespoon chia seeds / flaxseed powder
4 blocks ice

INSTRUCTIONS

1. Place all the ingredients in a blender and blend until smooth. Sprinkle with extra coconut sugar and a scoop of nut butter.

Summer Fruit Salad

Fantastic as a breakfast, a side salad and, of course, a dessert.
It is sweet, juicy and fabulously fresh. You can serve it with
banana ice cream, coconut whipped cream or simply as is.

INGREDIENTS
1 small melon
1 small papaya
2 nectarines
2 mangos
1 punnet (125 g) blueberries + extra to garnish
1 can (115 g) granadilla pulp

INSTRUCTIONS
1. Chill all the fruits before making the salad.
2. Peel the fruits and cut into 1-cm cubes.
3. Mix all the fruits, except the blueberries, and place into
   a glass salad bowl. Sprinkle with blueberries (keep the
   extra blueberries aside for later).
4. Cover the fruit salad in clingwrap until you are ready to
   serve it.
5. Just before unveiling your creation, pour the
   granadilla pulp over the fruits (do not mix), and
   add the extra blueberries.

Chickpea Omelette with Cashew-cream Sauce

INGREDIENTS

For the omelette

1 cup chickpea flour

1½ teaspoons garlic powder

1 teaspoon onion powder

¼ teaspoon turmeric

½ cup nutritional yeast

5 grinds kala namak (black Indian salt — optional)

¼ teaspoon bicarbonate of soda

1½ cups almond milk

Salt and pepper

Filling

Fried mushrooms, spinach, peppadews, green peppers, onion, tomatoes, meat-free strips or sausages, refried beans, fresh avocado, herbs.

For the sauce

½ cup cashews, soaked in hot water overnight (if you haven't soaked them, you can place the cashews in water and microwave them for 2 minutes)

1 cup almond milk

1 teaspoon garlic powder

1 teaspoon onion powder

Salt and pepper, to taste

Oil, for frying

NOTE: Use a non-stick pan with a lid.

INSTRUCTIONS

1. Place all the omelette ingredients in a food processor or blender and mix until smooth. Scrape down the sides from time to time. Prepare your filling ingredients and set aside to keep warm.

2. Make the sauce: Drain the cashews and place them in a blender (a high-speed blender or NutriBullet works fantastically well). Add the almond milk and spices and blend until the mixture reaches a smooth and creamy consistency. Set aside.

3. Make the rest of the omelette: Add ½ a tablespoon of oil in a non-stick pan. When you think it's hot, test the oil by adding a tiny drop of mixture into the pan. If the drop of batter bubbles profusely, the oil is ready. If using a 25-cm pan, add a ½ cup of the omelette mixture to the pan and swirl to ensure the liquid reaches all the pan edges. Close the pan with the lid. Let it cook over a low heat until small bubbles appear across the omelette's surface. Carefully flip the omelette and cook it on the other side for 5 more minutes. Slide you omelette onto a plate.

4. Add your filling, along with a serving of the cashew cream, to half the surface of the omelette. Carefully flip the other half over the filling to close the omelette.

5. Serve with crispy toast for breakfast or a side salad for lunch.

Tofu Scramble

This recipe comes courtesy of my best friend, Nina, who has cooked many of the recipes in this book with me. Tofu scramble is a fantastic alternative to the popular egg scramble and tastes every bit as good. To give the scramble an eggy taste, we add a sprinkle of kala namak — an Indian black salt that tastes just like boiled egg. You can fry up the tofu with assorted vegetables, including spinach, green and red peppers, mushrooms, tomatoes, asparagus, or even a vegan meat alternative.

INGREDIENTS

2 teaspoons vegetable oil
1 large onion, chopped
1 punnet mushrooms, sliced
¼ teaspoon salt
1 pack firm tofu, drained
2 to 3 tablespoons almond milk / 1 teaspoon Olé margarine
1 teaspoon turmeric
¼ teaspoon black salt (kala namak)
½ teaspoon of Ina Paarman's Garlic and Herb Seasoning
2 cups spinach, cored and chopped into chunks
6 peppadews, quartered
Salt and pepper, to taste
Baby spinach, to serve

INSTRUCTIONS

1. Heat 1 teaspoon of oil in a non-stick pan and fry the onion until translucent. Set aside.
2. In the same pan, fry the mushrooms by adding a sprinkle of salt and putting a lid on the pan until the mushrooms have released all their moisture. Remove the lid and simmer until all the liquid has evaporated. Set the mushrooms aside.
3. Crumble the tofu into pieces by hand or use a potato masher. Add the crumbled tofu to a clean pan, along with another teaspoon of oil, and fry for 1 minute, stirring constantly until it starts to brown. Add the almond milk or margarine if you're using this. Season with the spices and mix well. Add the cooked onion and mushrooms, as well as the chopped spinach and peppadews. Mix thoroughly. Season with salt and pepper.
4. Serve on seed bread toast with your favourite chutney and baby spinach leaves on top.

Smashed Beans & Creamy Avo Toast

This recipe is great for Saturday or Sunday-morning brunch — especially after a run.
It's packed with protein, fibre and essential vitamins and minerals, including calcium,
zinc, iron, folate, potassium, magnesium and B-complex vitamins. You can also use
the bean mixture as a nachos topping or a filling for wraps, burritos and enchiladas.

INGREDIENTS

1 tablespoon olive oil

1 onion, finely chopped

1 clove garlic, minced

1 teaspoon paprika

1 teaspoon ground cumin

½ teaspoon coriander

¼ teaspoon cayenne pepper

1 teaspoon dried parsley

1 teaspoon vegetable stock powder

½ can (200 g) cannellini beans in brine, drained
   and rinsed

½ can (200 g) Borlotti beans in brine, drained and rinsed

1 can (400 g) tomato and onion mix

1 tablespoon tomato paste

1 teaspoon Chipotle Tabasco (smoked tabasco)

1 tablespoon fresh parsley, chopped

½ lemon

1 avocado, pitted

Salt and pepper, to taste

1 tablespoon B-Well Creamy Gourmet mayonnaise

4 slices of toast / ciabatta

2 tablespoons spring onion, sliced

INSTRUCTIONS

1. Heat the olive oil in a pan over a high heat. Turn the heat down to low, add the onion and fry until translucent. Add the garlic and fry until slightly browned. Add all the spices and mix through the onion and garlic. Add the drained beans and mix through.

2. Smash some of the beans using a potato smasher. Add the tomato and onion mix, the tomato paste and the Chipotle Tabasco. Simmer over a low heat until the water from the tomato and onion mix has evaporated. Take off the heat; adjust the seasoning according to taste. Mix through the chopped parsley and a squeeze of lemon juice (keep half for the avocado). Set aside.

3. In a mixing bowl, mash the avocado with a fork. Add salt and pepper, the mayonnaise and lemon juice and mash further (you can also add more cayenne pepper if you like it spicy).

4. If using ciabatta, cut open the rolls, brush with olive oil and roast under the oven grill for a few minutes. If using toast, place your slices of bread in the toaster.

5. Spread a layer of creamy avocado over your bread of choice. Top with the bean mixture and garnish with scattered fresh spring onion.

Tropical Oats Bowl

INGREDIENTS

1 cup water

1 cup coconut milk

Pinch of salt

1 cup oats

¼ cup pistachio nuts

¼ cup dried banana

1½ cups fresh pineapple, chopped

½ teaspoon ground nutmeg

1 can (115 g) granadilla pulp

Juice and zest of 1 lime

1 tablespoon desiccated coconut / coconut flakes

INSTRUCTIONS

1. Bring the water and coconut milk to the boil. Add a pinch of salt. When bubbling, add the cup of oats and cook over a medium heat. Stir continuously until the oats are soft and half the liquid has been absorbed.
2. While the oats are cooking, dry-toast the pistachio nuts in a pan until slightly browned. Chop the pistachio nuts and dried banana and set aside.
3. Add 1 cup chopped pineapple and the nutmeg to the pan and fry over a medium heat. Add ¾ of the can granadilla pulp and the lemon juice and fry until slightly browned and sticky. Add the pineapple mixture to the pot of oats and stir through.
4. Dish the oats into two bowls.
5. Pour over the remaining granadilla pulp and sprinkle with coconut, chopped pistachios and banana, plus the remaining pineapple and lime zest. If you like your oats milky, add more of the coconut milk, too.

TIP

To add a healthier touch, use fresh granadillas instead of canned pulp. Other great tropical toppings include fresh (or dried) mango and banana chunks. Like your oats sweeter? Sprinkle over some coconut blossom sugar while the oats are cooking.

Chocolate Overnight Oats

This healthy breakfast is perfect for a rushed household. Make it within 5 minutes the night before, and simply grab your jar and enjoy it before jumping in the car. There are a myriad flavours, but chocolate has to be the ultimate.

INGREDIENTS

½ cup oats
2 tablespoons chia seeds
1 tablespoon flaxseeds
1 tablespoon cocoa powder
1 teaspoon vanilla essence
¼ teaspoon ground cinnamon
1 large, ripe banana, mashed
1 cup almond milk

Toppings
Fresh banana, peanut butter, cocoa nibs, toasted
   buckwheat, muesli

INSTRUCTIONS

1. Add all the dry ingredients to a mixing bowl and combine. Add the mashed banana and almond milk and mix well. Spoon into a glass jar, seal the jar and store in the fridge overnight.
2. Next morning, add my suggested toppings to your oats mixture and enjoy cold, or scoop into a bowl, warm in the microwave and enjoy hot.

Vegan Flapjacks

Have fun with the flapjacks by playing around with different toppings. Blend frozen mangos, strawberries and bananas for a delicious ice cream to scoop on top of your flapjacks. Or caramelise walnuts in maple syrup to give your flapjacks some crunch.

INGREDIENTS

1 cup + 1 tablespoon cake flour
1 tablespoon white sugar
2 teaspoons baking powder
Pinch of salt
2 tablespoons vegetable oil
1½ cups unsweetened soya milk

INSTRUCTIONS

1. Sift the flour, sugar, baking powder and salt in a big bowl. Add the vegetable oil and slowly add the soya milk to the bowl while mixing.
2. Mix the batter until it is smooth — try to eliminate all the flour lumps.
3. Heat a non-stick pan on the stove — when the pan is hot, turn the heat down to low.
4. Drop 3½ tablespoons of the batter at a time into the pan. When the surface of the flapjack is covered in bubbles, flip the flapjack to cook on the other side.
5. Place the cooked flapjack on a plate. Cover with another plate or a pot's lid to keep the flapjacks from getting cold.
6. Stack four to five pancakes on top of each other. Garnish with sauce and toppings of your choice. (See Chocolate sauce on page 183.)

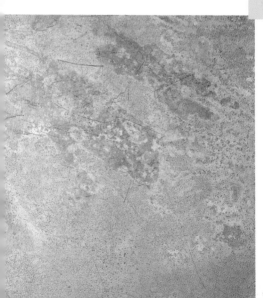

It's time
for
a snack

Crispy Roasted Chickpeas

Forget blue Doritos, roasted chickpeas are my favourite new party snack! Not only are they immensely tasty, but they are also much healthier than any potato crisp — and the varieties go on. Add spice with Tabasco and cayenne pepper, or sweeten with cinnamon and sugar. Soak them in vinegar before roasting to create a salt and vinegar flavour.

INGREDIENTS

1 can (400 g) chickpeas
4 tablespoons olive oil
1 to 2 teaspoons paprika
1 to 2 teaspoons ground cumin

INSTRUCTIONS

1. Preheat the oven to 180˚C.
2. Drain the chickpeas and rinse with water. Pat them dry with a dishcloth.
3. Place the chickpeas in an oven-proof dish and drizzle with 2 tablespoons olive oil and the spices. Mix well to combine, and spread out the chickpeas in a single layer.
4. After 30 minutes' oven time, remove and drizzle with the rest of the olive oil (and more spices if you wish). Mix through, and return to the oven for another 20 minutes. The chickpeas should be extremely crunchy and golden-brown when done, but watch out that they do not burn.

Makes 2 trays | 1 hour, 30 minutes

Crunchy Kale Chips

This new-generation chip is stealing the snack-scene spotlight. Kale chips are a delightful and healthy alternative to potato crisps, and easy to make. If you have a dehydrator, use this nifty equipment to dry out the leaves. The oven works perfectly fine, too. Since I love to spice things up, I add a few drops of Tabasco with the olive oil or I make my own mix of cumin, coriander and cayenne pepper. Or, make them cheesy by rubbing a tahini and nutritional-yeast mix onto the leaves before baking. What a great way to consume your daily dose of dark leafy greens!

INGREDIENTS

2 bunches curly kale
2 tablespoons olive oil
1 to 2 tablespoons of your preferred spice (I use Ina Paarman's Vegetable Spice)

INSTRUCTIONS

1. Preheat the oven to 100°C.
2. Wash the kale in cold, salted water. Tear off bite-sized pieces of kale leaves and place in a colander to drain. Discard the stems in your organic waste bin. Dry the kale bites completely using a dishcloth or a lettuce spinner.
3. Place them in a big mixing bowl and add the olive oil plus the spice. Massage the kale until all the pieces are covered.
4. Lay out the kale on baking trays, taking care not to place them on top of each other. You'll have to bake the kale in batches — place in the oven, but leave the oven door open slightly. Bake until crispy, turning the kale leaves over halfway. Repeat until done.
5. Serve instead of potato crisps, toss them into a salad or Buddha bowl or use inside wraps. They are best enjoyed immediately.

Spicy Tandoori Cauliflower Bites

INGREDIENTS

1 large cauliflower head

Cooking spray

1 tablespoon fresh coriander leaves / sliced
  spring onion

1 tablespoon olive oil

For the marinade

¾ cup coconut cream

2 to 4 teaspoons garam masala spice (depending
  on how spicy you like your food)

1 teaspoon paprika

1 teaspoon ground cumin

½ teaspoon ground cinnamon

1 tablespoon tomato paste

1 tablespoon lemon juice

1 tablespoon coconut-blossom sugar (or
  substitute with maple syrup or brown sugar)

1 teaspoon ginger paste

1 teaspoon minced garlic

INSTRUCTIONS

1. Preheat the oven to 200°C.
2. Wash and dry the cauliflower. Cut it into bite-sized pieces.
3. Mix all the marinade ingredients in a large mixing bowl.
4. Add the cauliflower pieces to the mixing bowl and coat well. Leave to marinate for 30 minutes.
5. Spray an oven-proof dish with cooking spray. Place the cauliflower bites in the oven-proof dish, drizzle with olive oil and bake for 30 minutes (turning the pieces over halfway and drizzling again) until you've cooked and beautifully browned the cauliflower.
6. Remove from the oven and place on a serving dish. Top with fresh coriander leaves or sliced spring onion.

Go-to, Oil-free Hummus

INGREDIENTS

1 can (400 g) drained and rinsed chickpeas (I prefer to use KOO)
2 heaped tablespoons tahini
3 tablespoons lemon juice
1 crushed garlic clove or ¾ teaspoon preserved garlic
3½ tablespoons water (use more if the consistency is too chunky for you)
1 teaspoon ground cumin
½ teaspoon ground turmeric
Pinch of salt and pepper

INSTRUCTIONS

1. Blend all the ingredients in a food processor or with a hand blender.
2. Serve with veggies, couscous, toast, as a dip for chips, in wraps, salads and on burgers.

Roasted Red-pepper Hummus

INGREDIENTS

2 cloves garlic, sliced in half
2 red peppers, seeded and cut in quarters
Olive oil
Grind of sea salt
1 can (400 g) chickpeas, drained
2 tablespoons tahini
3 tablespoons lemon juice
1 teaspoon paprika
¼ teaspoon cayenne pepper
Black pepper

INSTRUCTIONS

1. Preheat the oven to 200°C.
2. Prepare the vegetables. Place the garlic halves and red-pepper quarters in an oven-proof dish. Drizzle and rub with olive oil and a grind of salt. Place in the oven. Roast for about 20 minutes, until the red pepper is soft and starts to blacken on the sides.
3. Place all the ingredients in a food processor, along with the roasted red-pepper quarters and garlic halves. Blend until smooth.

Sundried Tomato Pesto

INGREDIENTS

1 packet of Woolworths' preserved sundried tomatoes in vinaigrette (make sure the vinaigrette isn't lemon flavoured)
1 clove garlic
2 tablespoons tomato paste
2 tablespoons lemon juice
½ red chilli, seeded
1 cup raw cashew nuts
Pinch of salt

INSTRUCTIONS

1. Place all the pesto ingredients in a blender and mix until smooth.

Pea Pesto

INGREDIENTS

1½ cups frozen peas

2 cloves garlic, left whole

3 tablespoons olive oil

2 to 3 tablespoons fresh lemon juice

½ cup cashew nuts / soaked sunflower seeds

½ green chilli, seeded

Good grind of salt and pepper

4 to 5 chopped mint leaves

1 teaspoon lemon zest

INSTRUCTIONS

1. Blanch the peas: Fill a mixing bowl with water and ice. Set aside. Bring a pot of water to the boil. Throw in the peas and cook for 10 minutes until bright green and slightly softened. Drain the peas and transfer to the mixing bowl filled with ice water. Drain again. Set aside.

2. Make the pesto: Place the cooked peas in a food processor. Add the garlic, olive oil, lemon juice, cashew nuts, chilli, salt and pepper, mint leaves and lemon zest to the food processor. Blend until smooth. Taste and adjust seasoning if needed.

Sweet & Creamy Basil Pesto

INGREDIENTS

¼ cup pine nuts

1 cup baby spinach

2 cups basil leaves

½ cup raw cashew nuts

3 tablespoons lemon juice

1 clove garlic

2 tablespoons olive oil

Salt and pepper

1 spring onion, chopped

1 tablespoon sweet-chilli sauce (optional)

INSTRUCTIONS

1. Dry-toast the pine nuts in a hot pan (do not add oil) until slightly browned. Swirl the nuts in the pan to prevent them from burning. Next, put them in the food processor (not a blender) with all the other ingredients. Process until you reach a smooth, pesto consistency. Remember, this pesto is creamier than usual so you'll need to process it longer. From time to time, scrape down the processor's sides. Taste and adjust the flavour with extra salt, pepper, lemon juice or sweet-chilli sauce. Serve as a dip, in wraps, on toasted bruschetta or with pasta.

Let's have a light lunch

Zucchini Noodle Soup

This simple summer soup not only bursts with flavour, it is also quick and easy.
It's super-healthy, too. It will fill your tummy, yet leave you feeling light and fresh.

INGREDIENTS

3 cups water
1 Knorr Vegetable Stock Pot
2 stalks celery, chopped
½ red pepper, seeded and chopped
1 teaspoon Robertsons Crushed Chillies (use less if you
   don't like it spicy)
⅓ cup fresh parsley, snipped
2 zucchinis, spiralised
Extra parsley, for garnish

INSTRUCTIONS

1. In a pot, bring the water (with the Stock Pot) to the boil.
Add the chopped celery, red pepper, chilli flakes and
parsley; boil for 3 minutes. Add the zucchini noodles
and boil for another 2 minutes.
2. Transfer to a bowl or serving dish and garnish with
fresh parsley leaves.

Couscous & Green Salad with Roasted Butternut and Beetroot

A big, beautiful salad to brighten up any table. This dish is a cinch to bring
to life, and counters every stigma about salads not being satisfying. A hit
with diners, it's a cut above your average mixed greens at a braai.

INGREDIENTS

1 medium butternut, peeled and cubed
1 bunch of beets, peeled and cubed (or 1 packet of sweet-and-sour beetroot)
2 tablespoons olive oil
Salt and pepper
1 cup whole-wheat couscous
1 cup boiled water
1 teaspoon Ina Paarman's Vegetable Seasoning
2 cups mixed greens (lettuce, baby spinach, rocket)
¼ cucumber, halved and sliced
10 cherry tomatoes
1 avocado, pitted and sliced
¼ cup blueberries
1 tablespoon dried cranberries
Crispy roasted chickpeas (see recipe on page 46)
¼ cup walnuts, broken into pieces
½ cup vegetable crisps

INSTRUCTIONS

1. Preheat the oven to 180°C.
2. Place the butternut and beetroot in an oven-proof dish, drizzle with olive oil and season with salt and pepper. Roast for 30 minutes until soft yet crispy.
3. Place the couscous in a bowl (with a lid), add the boiled water and close the lid. Leave to stand for 10 minutes, then fluff it with a fork. Sprinkle with the vegetable seasoning and mix through.
4. On a flat dish, spread out the couscous as a base. Top with the roasted butternut and beetroot — cover the couscous completely. Build a green salad on top of the butternut and beetroot using the greens, cucumber, tomatoes and avocado. Sprinkle blueberries, cranberries, roasted chickpeas and walnuts over your creation. Finally, place a handful of vegetable crisps on top.
5. Serve with your favourite vinaigrette.

Earthy Brown-rice Medley

INGREDIENTS

1 cup brown lentils

4 teaspoons Ina Paarman's Beef Flavour Stock Powder

4 cups boiled water

1 cup brown rice

1 punnet mushrooms, quartered

1 head broccoli, chopped into small pieces

1 teaspoon olive oil

Braai spice

1 tablespoon olive oil

3 onions, sliced in rings

INSTRUCTIONS

1. Preheat the oven to 180˚C.
2. Rinse the lentils until the water runs clean. Mix the stock powder with the boiled water. Bring the stock water, rice and lentils to a boil. Once it is bubbling profusely, lower the heat, cover with a lid and simmer for 40 minutes. Stir through once or twice during the cooking process to prevent the rice from burning.
3. Add the mushroom quarters and broccoli pieces to an oven-proof dish. Drizzle the vegetables with olive oil and add a grind of braai spice. Roast in the oven for 30 minutes. Mix halfway through. While the rice and lentils are cooking, and the mushrooms and broccoli are roasting, add 1 tablespoon of oil to a hot, non-stick pan. Add the onions and turn down the heat to the lowest possible setting. Cook the onions over a low heat until caramelised, stirring continuously. Add a teaspoon of water every now and then to help the process along.
4. Remove the rice and lentil mix. Strain well. Remove the broccoli and mushrooms. Mix into the caramelised onions, rice and lentils and serve hot.

Serves 8 | 45 minutes

Multigrain Salad

INGREDIENTS

1 cup cooked red quinoa
1 cup cooked buckwheat
1 cup brown lentils, cooked
½ cucumber, cubed
1 tomato, cubed
½ red onion, chopped
2 tablespoons fresh parsley

For the dressing

3 tablespoons tahini
5 tablespoons lemon juice
¼ cup water
2 tablespoons white-wine vinegar
1 teaspoon Ina Paarman's Garlic & Herb Seasoning
Pinch of salt

INSTRUCTIONS.

1. Cook the quinoa and buckwheat according to the packet instructions.
2. Mix the grains with the lentils, cucumber, tomato, red onion and fresh parsley.
3. Place all the dressing ingredients in a mixing bowl and mix until smooth.
4. Pour the dressing over the salad and mix through.

Pea & Pesto Quinoa Salad

INGREDIENTS

2½ cups frozen peas
2 cloves garlic, left whole
3 tablespoons olive oil
2 tablespoons fresh lemon juice
½ cup cashew nuts
½ green chilli, seeded
½ cup Orley Whip, for dressings
Good grind of salt and pepper
4 to 5 chopped mint leaves
1 teaspoon lemon zest
1 cup quinoa
2 cups baby spinach
1 cup rocket
1 tablespoon chopped mint
1½ cups shredded purple cabbage

TIP

For extra crunch, dry-roast a few pine nuts or hazelnuts in a pan and sprinkle on top. For saltiness, add capers.

INSTRUCTIONS

1. Blanch the peas: Fill a mixing bowl with water and ice. Set aside. Bring a pot of water to the boil. As soon as the water is boiling, throw in the peas and cook for 10 minute, until the peas are bright green and slightly softened. Drain the peas and transfer to the mixing bowl filled with ice water. Drain again. Set aside the peas.

2. Make the pesto sauce: Place 1½ cups of the cooked peas in a food processor (keep the extra cup of peas for the salad). Add the garlic, olive oil, lemon juice, cashew nuts, chilli, Orley Whip, salt and pepper, mint leaves and lemon zest to the food processor. Blend until smooth. Taste and adjust the seasoning to your liking. Set aside.

3. Cook the quinoa: Rinse the quinoa under cold running water, using a sieve, until the water is clear. If you don't rinse the quinoa properly, it will have a bitter taste. The consistency will be stodgy, not fluffy. Transfer the quinoa to a saucepan or pot, add 2 cups of water and a pinch of salt. Bring the quinoa to a boil. Once boiling, reduce the heat and simmer for 15 minutes until all the liquid is absorbed and the quinoa has sprouted. Allow the quinoa to cool down, then fluff with a fork.

4. Assemble the salad: In a glass salad bowl, add half the baby spinach, followed by half the rocket, the mint and purple cabbage. Pour half the pea-pesto sauce onto the salad mix. Layer half the quinoa on top and sprinkle with half the leftover peas. Repeat the above layers: baby spinach, rocket, mint, cabbage, pesto sauce, quinoa, peas.

Fresh Chicken-style Salad Cups

INGREDIENTS

1 butter lettuce, to use as cups

250 g pasta of choice

1 teaspoon oil, for frying

1 pack (380 g) Fry's chicken-style strips, defrosted
   and cut into 1-cm chunks

1 teaspoon chicken spice

1 red apple, cored and cubed (squeeze over lemon juice
   so it doesn't brown)

1 green apple, cored and grated (squeeze over lemon
   juice so it doesn't brown)

2 sprigs of celery, finely sliced

2 sprigs of spring onion, finely sliced

Zest of 1 lemon (only grate the yellow skin,
   none of the white)

1 tablespoon fresh dill, chopped, for garnish

1 tablespoon sesame seeds, for garnish

For the sauce

150 g silken tofu, drained, but not pressed

½ cup almond milk

1 tablespoon apple-cider vinegar

½ tablespoon lemon juice

2 teaspoons Dijon mustard

1 tablespoon maple syrup (or sugar)

Sea salt and pepper, to taste

INSTRUCTIONS

1. Wash the lettuce head, drain the water and cut into lettuce cups. Cook the pasta according to the packet instructions (about 12 to 15 minutes), drain and set aside to cool.
2. Heat the olive oil in a non-stick pan. Add the Fry's chicken-style chunks and chicken spice. Fry until the chunks are golden-brown. Set aside to cool.
3. Mix all the salad ingredients in a mixing bowl (excluding the dill and sesame seeds).
4. Place all the sauce ingredients in a blender or food processor and blend until smooth. Remember to taste and season accordingly with sea salt and black pepper. Add the sauce ingredients to the mixing bowl and stir to mix.
5. Keep a little sauce aside to add just before serving. Place the mixing bowl in the fridge for the salad to cool and flavours to combine. When ready to serve, mix through the additional sauce and transfer the salad into the lettuce cups. Sprinkle with the chopped dill and sesame seeds.

Oriental Stir-Fry
with Crispy 'Chicken' & Satay Sauce

Their chicken-style pieces are among my favourite products from The Fry Family Food Co. range. They are hugely versatile and can replace chicken in almost every pasta or stew-style dish. I always have a box in the freezer. For this recipe, you can also use the chicken-style burger patties or schnitzels, baked in the oven and cut into strips.

INGREDIENTS

1 box (380 g) Fry's Chicken-style Strips, defrosted

1 packet noodles of choice (rice noodles, spaghetti, whole-wheat, pulse pasta)

1 packet (500 g) mixed oriental stir-fry vegetables (preferably fresh, but frozen will work)

1 lemon, cut in quarters (used in different parts of the recipe)

Fresh coriander, for garnish

For the peanut satay sauce

3 tablespoons peanut butter, unsalted and sugar-free

5 tablespoons soya sauce

2 teaspoons apple-cider vinegar

2 teaspoons maple syrup

1 fresh chilli, seeded and chopped

1 tablespoon fresh coriander, chopped

2 teaspoons fresh ginger, grated

5 to 6 tablespoons water

Juice from ¼ lemon (from the 1 lemon under 'ingredients')

For the stir-fry sauce

6 tablespoons soya sauce

1 tablespoon apple-cider vinegar

1 glove garlic, minced

2 teaspoons fresh ginger, grated

1 tablespoon maple syrup

¼ teaspoon sriracha sauce

Juice of ½ lemon (from the 1 lemon under 'ingredients')

2 teaspoons brown sugar

INSTRUCTIONS

1. Fry the chicken-style strips in a teaspoon of oil until brown and crispy.
2. Cook the noodles according to the packet instructions.
3. Place all the satay sauce ingredients in a mixing bowl and whisk until you reach a smooth, but runny sauce consistency. Add more water if needed. Pour into a ramekin or sauce jar. Top with chopped coriander (optional).
4. Mix the stir-fry sauce ingredients together. Heat a bit of oil in a wok and add the stir-fry vegetables. Fry over a high heat for 5 minutes. Add the stir-fry sauce and fry the vegetables until tender, but not too limp. Season to taste. Remove from the heat and add a squeeze of the last ¼ lemon.
5. Dish up your meal: Place one portion of noodles in a bowl, top with the vegetables and a bit of the stir-fry sauce. Tower the chicken-style strips on top of the stir-fry vegetables and garnish with coriander.
6. Serve with the peanut satay sauce on the side.

Lasagne

A lasagne without lasagne sheets. I grew up with this family-favourite dish — for as long as I can remember, we used bright-green spinach tagliatelle instead. Our clan has passed this recipe down the generations. When I finally received it, I had no choice but to veganise the ingredients and carry on the tradition. Eating lasagne has always been a special occasion in our home — never eaten in front of the television and never served without crispy garlic bread, a big green salad and a bottle of Cabernet Sauvignon.

INGREDIENTS

For the mince

1 teaspoon B-Well Canola Oil, for frying
1 white onion, chopped
1 teaspoon garlic, minced
2 x 380 g Fry's Meat-free Mince
Pinch of salt
1 gravy sachet (comes with Fry's mince)
½ teaspoon Robertsons Mixed Herbs
½ teaspoon Robertsons Dried Origanum
1 teaspoon fresh rosemary leaves, chopped
4 dried bay leaves
1 can (400 g) Miami tomato, basil, garlic and origanum
   (or use regular chopped tomato and onion mix)
50 g tomato paste

500 g egg-free tagliatelle
1 tablespoon B-Well Canola Oil
½ green pepper, seeded and chopped
1 tomato, sliced into 8 thin rings
1 packet Knorr Thick White Onion Soup
800 ml unsweetened soya milk
1 teaspoon cornstarch
60 ml unsweetened soya milk (to mix with cornstarch)
1 cup Violife for Pizza vegan cheese, grated

INSTRUCTIONS

1. Heat the oil in a pan. Add the onion and fry until translucent. Add the garlic and fry until slightly browned. Take off the heat.

2. Add the mince and mix through the onion and garlic mixture. Add salt to taste. Put back on the heat and turn to medium. Add the gravy spice, mixed herbs, origanum and rosemary. Add the bay leaves to the pan. Fry until all the mince is cooked. Add the can of chopped tomato and mix through. Add the tomato paste and cook through. Remove from the heat and set aside. (Taste your mince mix: every tomato and onion-mix tastes different.)

3. Preheat the oven to 180°C. Cut the green pepper into small cubes, set aside.

4. Cook the pasta according to instructions. Drain with cold water and drizzle with the oil, Set aside.

5. Mix the cornstarch with the 60 ml unsweetened soya milk until dissolved and set aside. In a saucepan, mix the onion-soup powder with 800 ml room temperature soya milk until you've dissolved all the powder. Place on high heat and bring to a boil. Lower the heat and simmer the mixture, add the cornstarch mixture and cook until the sauce is thick, whisking continuously. Remove from heat and set aside.

6. Spray an oven-proof dish with cooking spray. Spread one layer of tagliatelle on the bottom. Add a layer of mince mix. Sprinkle ½ of the green pepper over the mince mix. Repeat: pasta, mince, green pepper.

7. Pour the sauce evenly over the dish. Sprinkle the cheese on top. Add slices of tomato as garnish (1 per block). Bake for 20 to 30 minutes at 180°C.

Chilli Con 'Carne'

This recipe tastes just as good without the soya mince.

INGREDIENTS

1 cup dried soya mince
1 red onion, chopped
1 cup of vegetable stock
1 teaspoon garlic, crushed
2 teaspoons onion powder
1 teaspoon smoked paprika
1 teaspoon turmeric
1 tin (400 g) chopped tomatoes
1 tin (400 g) black beans in brine / 2 cups cooked black
   soya beans
Salt and pepper, to taste
1 tin (410 g) whole corn, drained and panfried until
   charred slightly
1 teaspoon chilli flakes (more if you want a harder kick)
½ cup tomato purée

INSTRUCTIONS

1. Soak the soya mince in water for 20 minutes.
2. Drain the water and squeeze out the excess water.
3. In a large pot, fry the chopped red onion in a bit of the stock over a very low heat until soft and sweet. Add the garlic and spices: onion powder, paprika, and turmeric. Add a bit more of the stock and mix well to create a paste in the pot. Add the tin of chopped tomatoes and the black beans. Let it simmer on the stove over a low heat. Add salt and pepper to taste. Add the corn, chilli flakes and tomato purée. Stir well.
4. Add the soya mince and the rest of the stock, turning up the heat to medium. Stir occasionally until all the water is absorbed and the soya mince is soft — about 15 minutes. Taste and adjust the seasoning if necessary. I like adding more onion powder and chilli flakes.
5. Serve hot with a starch (cooked rice, mash potato, couscous or samp corn) or with steamed veggies.

Gary te Roller's Spaghetti Bolognaise

Gary te Roller is a plant-based health coach, wellness advocate, foodie and endurance athlete.

INGREDIENTS

For the sauce

1 red onion, finely chopped

1 punnet white mushrooms, finely chopped

3 cloves garlic, minced

½ head broccoli, finely chopped

2 large carrots, grated

1 cup brown lentils, uncooked

500 g chopped tomatoes — the reddest ones you can find

½ cup vegan sundried tomato pesto

1 tablespoon tomato paste

Handful fresh parsley

1 tablespoon dried thyme

2 teaspoons Himalayan salt

Handful fresh basil

Spices and herbs (½ teaspoon of each or more, according to your taste):

Cayenne pepper

Paprika

Turmeric

Herb salt

Ground coriander

1 packet (500 g) whole-wheat pasta

2 bags of zucchini spaghetti

INSTRUCTIONS

1. In a saucepan or pot, dry-fry the onion and mushrooms. Once you've browned the onions and mushroom, add the garlic, broccoli, carrots, uncooked lentils, chopped tomatoes, vegan sundried tomato pesto, tomato paste and 2 cups boiling water. Bring to a simmer for 20 minutes.

2. Add the parsley, thyme, salt, basil and spices. Allow to simmer with the lid on for another 25 minutes. Or leave it to simmer for longer. My rule is: the longer everything simmers, the more mature the flavours become — just how my gran spent the entire afternoon making spaghetti bolognaise. While simmering, boil a pot of water and add in a packet of whole-wheat pasta (a great test to ensure that this is, indeed, whole-wheat is by looking at the pasta label and dividing the carb by fibre content — the answer should be below 5).

3. Cook the pasta according to the packet instructions. During the last 5 minutes, add the bags of zucchini pasta. When the pasta is cooked, drain and set aside.

4. Serve the pasta with a generous dollop of the pasta sauce.

TIP

Add nutritional yeast to give the spaghetti bolognaise a cheesy taste.

Jessica Kotlowitz's Curried Soya Mince

Jessica Kotlowitz is the Green Dietitian. Keep up to date on her plant-loving foodie news at thegreendietitian.co.za.

INGREDIENTS

1 cup dried soya mince / textured vegetable protein

2 cups boiling water mixed with 2 teaspoons of Ina Paarman's Beef-flavour Stock Powder

1 onion, roughly chopped

2 cloves garlic, crushed

1 large carrot, diced

Sprinkling cumin seeds

3 bay leaves

4 teaspoons mild curry powder

1 (extra) teaspoon Ina Paarman's Beef-flavour Stock Powder

Chilli sauce, to taste

3 tablespoons peach chutney

1 baby white cabbage, shredded

INSTRUCTIONS

1. Soak the soya mince in the beef stock for 20 to 45 minutes until most of the water has been absorbed.

2. Sauté the onion and garlic in water until translucent. Add the carrots. Sauté for another 2 minutes. Add the cumin seeds, bay leaves, curry powder, extra teaspoon of stock powder, chilli sauce, chutney and rehydrated soya mince (along with the remaining soaking water). Turn down the heat and cover and simmer for 10 minutes.

3. Add the cabbage and simmer for a further 10 to 15 minutes or until the carrots are cooked through, stirring regularly to prevent burning. Right before serving, remove the bay leaves.

4. Serve in a baked potato, with rice or on a piece of whole-wheat toast, along with a fresh green salad.

Rich Red-wine Mushroom Pasta

Another favourite Manic Monday meal ...

INGREDIENTS

250 g whole-wheat pasta (or pasta of choice)

Oil, for frying

1 onion, chopped

2 cloves garlic, minced

1 teaspoon paprika

1 teaspoon dried origanum

¼ teaspoon ground cinnamon

1 punnet mushrooms, sliced

1 can (410 g) Miami tomato, basil, garlic and origanum

½ cup red wine

1 tablespoon tomato paste

4 teaspoons brown sugar

Salt and pepper, to taste

Nutritional yeast or vegan Parmesan cheese (optional)

INSTRUCTIONS

1. Cook the pasta according to the packet instructions. Drain and set aside.
2. Heat the oil in a non-stick pan over a low heat. Add the onion and cook until translucent. Add the garlic and cook until slightly brown. Add the paprika, origanum and cinnamon and coat the onions and garlic.
3. Add the mushrooms, plus a grind of salt to release the water from the mushrooms. Mix well and fry until brown. Once browned, pour in the can of tomatoes, red wine, tomato paste and brown sugar. Mix well to combine and simmer over a medium heat for 10 minutes.
4. Season with salt and pepper according to taste. Return the pasta to the pot with a bit of water and add the tomato-sauce mixture. Heat through thoroughly.
5. Dish into pasta bowls and serve with a sprinkle of nutritional yeast or grated vegan Parmesan cheese.

Mediterranean Pesto Pasta

INGREDIENTS

For the basil pesto

1 cup of sunflower seeds, soaked in hot water
   for an hour
2 packed cups baby spinach
1½ packed cups basil leaves, thick stems removed
1 clove garlic
Juice of 4½ lemons (about 4 tablespoons)
½ avocado, pitted and chopped
2 tablespoons nutritional yeast (optional)
1 tablespoon olive oil
Salt and pepper, to taste

For the pasta

1 box (250 g) Happy Earth People Red Lentil Pasta (or
   use any pasta)
1 tablespoon olive oil
1 white onion, chopped
1 clove garlic, minced
1 teaspoon paprika
1 teaspoon cayenne pepper
1 punnet button mushrooms, sliced
½ cup white wine (optional)
1 teaspoon mixed herbs
1 bunch spinach, cored and shredded into strips
6 sundried tomatoes or 15 cherry tomatoes, cut in half
Juice of ½ lemon (about 1 tablespoon)
Salt and pepper, to taste
15 Kalamata black olives, pitted and halved
2 tablespoons nutritional yeast (optional)
½ avocado, pitted and sliced, for garnish
Fresh rocket, for garnish

INSTRUCTIONS

1. Make the basil pesto: Drain the sunflower seeds and add all the ingredients to a food processor. Blend until it reaches a pesto consistency (very fine, but not completely smooth). Set aside.
2. Make the rest of the dish: Cook the pasta according to the packet instructions, drain and set aside. Add the olive oil (or water if you prefer) to a big wok. When hot, add the chopped onion and minced garlic. Add the paprika and cayenne pepper and coat the onion mixture.
3. When the onions are soft, add the mushrooms, white wine and mixed herbs. When the mushrooms turn brown, add the chopped spinach, tomatoes, squeeze of lemon juice and salt and pepper. Cook until the spinach turns bright green. Add the Kalamata olives and nutritional yeast, and stir through.
4. Add the pasta and basil pesto to the wok, and stir through.
5. Serve with avocado and fresh rocket on top.

It's
tea time

Pretty-in-Pink
Banana & Raspberry Muffins

INGREDIENTS

1 flax egg (1 tablespoon flaxseed powder,
   mixed with 3 tablespoons water)
2 very ripe bananas
½ cup almond milk
½ cup coconut oil, melted
1 teaspoon vanilla essence
1½ cups flour
¾ cup sugar
2 teaspoons baking powder
½ teaspoon bicarbonate of soda
¼ teaspoon salt
160 g raspberries, halved

INSTRUCTIONS

1. Preheat the oven to 180°C.
2. Line a muffin pan with paper cups.
3. In a small bowl, mix 1 tablespoon flaxseed powder with
   3 tablespoons water and allow to stand for 3 minutes.
4. Mash the bananas in a big mixing bowl. Add the
   almond milk, melted coconut oil, vanilla essence and
   flax-egg mixture and stir to mix well.
5. In a separate mixing bowl, sift the flour, sugar, baking
   powder, bicarbonate of soda and salt.
6. Gently mix the wet into the dry ingredients. Add the
   raspberries and fold in. Do not over-mix the batter.
7. Scoop 2 tablespoons of batter into each paper cup.
   Bake for 25 minutes — the 'ready' test is sticking a
   toothpick into the centre of the muffin. If it comes out
   clean, they are ready.
8. Remove from the oven and let it cool completely.
   Serve warm or cold with vegan margarine and
   raspberry jam.

Britney Varley's
Soya & Cider Scones

Britney Varley is a vegan chef at WILD — Plant-based Alchemy catering in Cape Town.

INGREDIENTS

2 teaspoons apple-cider vinegar

1 cup unsweetened soya milk

2 cups cake flour (preferably stone-ground)

4 teaspoons baking powder

½ teaspoon baking soda

1¼ teaspoons salt

½ cup coconut oil (refrigerate until solid, if not
    so already)

Olive oil, for basting

INSTRUCTIONS

1. Preheat the oven to 200°C.
2. Mix the apple-cider vinegar into the soya milk. Let it stand for a few minutes. In a large mixing bowl, mix the flour, baking powder, baking soda and salt. Break the solid coconut oil into pieces. Mix it into the flour with your hands and work it through until you are left with small pieces of coconut oil. Handle the dough quite quickly so that the heat from your hands does not melt the coconut oil.
3. You want whole, small pieces of coconut oil in the dough. This will create the scones' flakiness. Add the soya milk and apple-cider vinegar to the bowl. Stir until well combined and you have a dough mound. If the dough is too sticky, add 1 or 2 more tablespoons of flour at a time and mix in.
4. Place the dough onto a floured surface; fold the dough over onto itself and knead. Roll the dough to a 2½-cm thickness. Cut rounds with a cookie cutter. Place the rounds on a baking tray lined with baking paper. Leave space between the scones so that they have enough room to expand. Baste with olive oil.
5. Bake for 10 to 12 minutes until golden and cooked through.

Sweet Butternut Tart

INGREDIENTS

B-Well Canola Baking Spray (Blissful Bake)

For the crust

1 cup all-purpose flour

1 teaspoon baking powder

¼ teaspoon salt

1 teaspoon Orgran no-egg powder

3 tablespoons water

¼ cup Olé margarine

¼ cup caster sugar

1½ tablespoons almond milk

2 extra tablespoons all-purpose flour

For the filling

¾ cup brown sugar

5 tablespoons cornstarch

1 teaspoon ground cinnamon

¼ teaspoon ground nutmeg

¼ teaspoon ground ginger

1½ cups cooked butternut, puréed till smooth

2 cups almond milk

3 teaspoons Orgran no-egg powder

6 tablespoons water

1 tablespoon margarine

½ teaspoon vanilla essence

INSTRUCTIONS

1. Preheat the oven to 180°C.
2. Spray an oven-proof dish with cooking spray.
3. Make the crust: Sift the flour, baking powder and salt into a mixing bowl. Mix the Orgran powder and water together. Mix the margarine and sugar together using an electric mixer. Add the almond milk and Orgran egg mixture while the mixer is running. Add the dry ingredients (1 tablespoon at a time) to the wet ingredients while the mixture is running. Let it form a sticky dough. Scoop up the dough in your hands, add the additional 2 tablespoons of flour and press together to form a manageable dough. It should not stick to your hands. Add flour to a dry surface, roll out the dough and then press the dough down into the bottom of the dish. Set aside.
4. Make the filling: Mix the brown sugar with the cornstarch, cinnamon, nutmeg and ginger. Add the butternut and almond milk to the dry ingredients and mix through. Transfer the mixture to a pot and cook over a low heat until it starts to thicken. Mix the Orgran with the water until dissolved and add to the pot mixture. Add the margarine and the vanilla essence.
5. Pour the mixture into the dish and bake for 30 minutes.
6. Remove from the oven and allow to cool completely.
7. Cut into squares and enjoy.

Milk Tart

INGREDIENTS

B-Well Canola Baking Spray (Blissful Bake)

Wax paper

For the crust

1 cup all-purpose flour

1 teaspoon baking powder

¼ teaspoon salt

1 teaspoon Orgran no-egg powder

3 tablespoons water

¼ cup Olé margarine

¼ cup caster sugar

1½ tablespoons almond milk

2 extra tablespoons all-purpose flour

For the filling

5 tablespoons cornstarch

1 litre unsweetened almond milk

6 tablespoons sugar

1 cinnamon stick

1 teaspoon vanilla essence

Sprinkle of ground nutmeg and cinnamon

Extra

Beans or chickpeas to use as baking beads, if you don't
have baking beads.

INSTRUCTIONS

1. Preheat the oven to 180°C.
2. Spray an oven-proof dish with cooking spray.
3. Cut the wax paper to fit into an oven-proof dish (turn
   the dish around on the wax paper, trace and cut).
4. Make the crust: Sift the flour, baking powder and salt
   into a mixing bowl.
5. Mix the Orgran powder and water together.
6. Mix the margarine and sugar together using an
   electric mixer. Add the almond milk and Orgran
   egg mixture while the mixer is running.
7. Add the dry ingredients (1 tablespoon at a time)
   to the wet ingredients while the mixture is running.
   Let it form a sticky dough.
8. Scoop up the dough in your hands, add the additional
   2 tablespoons of flour and press together to form a
   manageable dough. It should not stick to your hands.
9. Add flour to a dry surface, roll out the dough and then
   press the dough down into the bottom of the dish.
10. Bake for 5 minutes at 180°C, using the baking beans.
    Remove from the oven and set aside.
11. Make the filling: Mix the cornstarch with 1 cup of the
    almond milk. Whisk until completely dissolved.
12. Add the rest of the almond milk (3 cups) to a pot
    along with the sugar and cinnamon stick. Bring the
    mixture to the boil, stirring continuously.
13. Once it is boiling, turn down the heat to low and let
    the mixture simmer.
14. Slowly add the rest of the almond milk with the corn-
    starch and the vanilla essence to the pot. Continue
    to stir.
15. Simmer the mixture until it becomes thick, about
    20 minutes, stirring continuously.
16. Remove the cinnamon stick and pour the filling
    onto the baked pastry. Sprinkle with cinnamon
    and nutmeg.
17. Place in the oven and bake for 30 minutes.
18. Remove from the oven and allow to cool. Transfer the
    milk tart to the fridge to set for 1 hour.

Britney Varley's
Gluten-free Banana Bread

INGREDIENTS

1½ cups chickpea flour

1¼ teaspoons ground cinnamon

½ teaspoon salt

1 teaspoon baking powder

1 teaspoon baking soda

4 tablespoons xylitol (or 4 tablespoons brown sugar)

½ cup dark vegan chocolate chips (optional)

2 tablespoons flaxseed powder (combine with 5 tablespoons of water and let stand for 5 minutes to make
flax egg)

2 teaspoons vanilla essence

1 teaspoon apple-cider vinegar

4 tablespoons coconut oil, melted and cooled

4 to 5 bananas, mashed well (depending on size:
4 if large, 5 if small)

INSTRUCTIONS

1. Preheat the oven to 180°C.

2. Combine the chickpea flour, cinnamon, salt, baking
powder, baking soda and xylitol in a large bowl and
mix. Add the flax egg, vanilla essence, apple-cider
vinegar and coconut oil to the bowl of mashed banana
and mix. Now combine all the ingredients and mix well
with a wooden spoon until completely blended.

3. Prepare a bread pan with cooking spray. The mixture
fills a 21 cm x 11 cm x 6 cm pan completely, so don't go
for anything smaller; or you'll have to split the mixture
into two pans and bake it for less time. Pour the mixture into the bread pan and bake for 40 to 45 minutes.

4. Using a knife or toothpick, test to see whether it comes
out dry. (See Note below.)

NOTE that using a knife or toothpick to test doesn't
always work straight away with banana bread — the
banana can remain quite wet until the bread has completely cooled down. If you find that your banana bread
needs to go in longer after it has cooled, simply put it
back into the oven at the same temperature for about
5 minutes.

Thyme, Cinnamon & Orange Sponge

I recently enjoyed the most delicious gin cocktail, Ambition Remedy, at the Secret Gin Bar in Wale Street, Cape Town. The fresh thyme, cucumber and cinnamon complemented this elderflower gin and tonic beautifully. That flavour combination played with my palate ever since. Stuck in traffic one day, I was munching on a naartjie while dreaming about that delightful drink. Penetrating my reverie, the overwhelming citrus fragrance inspired the idea of an orange, thyme and cinnamon sponge cake. After making an ingredient pitstop, I breathed my dream to life. This cake is light, fluffy and dreamy. Fresh lemon zest cuts through the sweetness and a subtle hint of thyme infuses the final product with an earthy aroma.

INGREDIENTS

B-Well Canola Baking Spray (Blissful Bake)

For the cake

2 cups Almond Breeze Unsweetened Almond Milk
1¾ cups cake wheat flour
1 cup white sugar
1 teaspoon bicarbonate of soda
½ teaspoon salt
1 teaspoon ground cinnamon
1 teaspoon dried thyme
2 teaspoons orange extract
⅓ cup olive oil
1 tablespoon white-wine vinegar

For the frosting

2½ cups icing sugar
3 tablespoons vegan margarine
2 tablespoons almond milk
3 teaspoons orange extract
Zest of 1 orange

NOTE The ingredients for the cake can be doubled to make a 4-tier cake.

INSTRUCTIONS

1. Preheat the oven to 180°C. Spray a 20-cm round cake tin with cooking spray.
2. Place the almond milk in a pot with 2 cinnamon sticks and a few fresh springs of thyme. Bring the milk to the boil and then turn down the heat. Let the almond milk simmer for 15 minutes to infuse the flavours.
3. Sift the dry ingredients into a mixing bowl. Remove the infused almond milk from the stove and mix 1⅓ cups of the milk with the rest of the wet ingredients in another mixing bowl. Whisk the wet into dry ingredients until you've combined them well.
4. Pour the cake mixture into the tin and tap the tin on the kitchen counter to remove any air bubbles. Bake the cake for 30 minutes.
5. While the cake bakes, prepare the frosting: Add the icing sugar, vegan margarine, almond milk and orange extract into a mixing bowl. Use an electric mixer to mix the frosting until smooth and creamy. The consistency of the frosting must be thin enough to spread evenly over the cake, but thick enough for it not to slide off the cake. If it is too thin, add more icing sugar. Too thick? Add more almond milk. When the cake is completely cool, spread the frosting over the cake. Decorate with lemon zest and fresh thyme.
6. Remove the cake from the oven and insert a cake tester into the centre of the cake. A clean tester means your cake is done. Move to a cooling rack to cool completely.

Hoppy's Chocolate & Coconut Tart

Amy Hopkins is the food editor of *Women's Health SA*. She is also a runner, yogi and Green Monday ambassador. This amazingly easy dessert is not only vegan, but is also gluten-free. It's a favourite among her friends and family. Keep it in the fridge in-between servings. It's also weight-loss friendly because it's really rich. That is, you only need a slither to get your sweet fix.

INGREDIENTS

1 teaspoon coconut oil
⅓ cup desiccated coconut
1 can (400 ml) coconut cream
200 g Lindt 90% dark chocolate or any other good-quality, dairy-free dark chocolate, broken into small pieces
200 g strawberries or raspberries
Extra coconut flakes, for garnishing (optional)
1 tablespoon icing sugar, for sprinkling (optional)

INSTRUCTIONS

1. Grease a tart dish or small, springform cake tin with the coconut oil. Sprinkle desiccated coconut evenly over the bottom of the tart dish and a bit up the sides of the dish, too. Pour the coconut cream into a saucepan, set over a low heat. Add the chocolate and stir slowly until melted and combined.
2. Pour the chocolate mixture into the tart dish and place in the fridge to set for a few hours or overnight. Remove the tart from the fridge just before serving, decorate with berries, coconut flakes and a sprinkle of icing sugar.

NOTE Keep it seasonal by changing it up in winter. Grate the zest of one orange into the coconut mixture and serve with toasted almond flakes instead of berries. Serve with extra rinds of orange zest.

Hein van Tonder's Vegan Fruit Cake

Hein van Tonder is a food photographer, stylist, recipe developer
and blogger. This is a rich and very moist cake, packed with flavour.

INGREDIENTS

150 g dried prunes, chopped
500 g prepacked dried-fruit cake mix
100 g raisins
100 g sultanas
200 g glace cherries
175 g coconut oil
300 g dark muscovado sugar
⅗ cup coffee liqueur
Juice and zest of 2 oranges
2 tablespoons cacao
2 teaspoons mixed spice
1 teaspoon instant espresso powder
½ teaspoon salt
45 ml flaxseed powder
⅖ cup water
175 g flour
100 g ground almonds
100 g applesauce
100 g mixed nuts of your choice, roughly
   chopped (optional)
1 teaspoon baking powder
⅖ cup brandy, rum or amaretto
Extra brandy or rum, for brushing during resting

INSTRUCTIONS

1. Place the fruit, coconut oil, sugar, liqueur, orange juice
   and zest, cacao, mixed spice, espresso powder and
   salt in a saucepan. Bring to a slow boil while stirring.
   Simmer for 10 minutes, remove from the heat and let it
   stand to reach room temperature.

2. Preheat the oven to 150°C. Line the sides and bottom
   of a 22-cm loose-bottom cake tin with baking paper.
   Double-line the sides of the tin with baking paper,
   making sure the paper is about 3 cm higher than the
   edges of the tin.

3. In a large bowl, add the flaxseed powder and water,
   mix and let it stand to thicken for a few minutes. Add
   the fruit, flour, almonds, applesauce, nuts (if using),
   baking powder to the flax mixture and mix well. Spoon
   the mixture into the prepared tin and bake for about
   2 hours or more until the cake is firm and the top is
   quite shiny. Start testing the cake after 1 hour, 45 minutes by inserting a cake tester into the centre.

4. Don't worry if there is a very slight bit of moist batter
   attached to the tester — as long as the batter isn't raw.
   If it is too uncooked, return to the oven for another
   15 minutes. Test again and repeat if needed, until
   the cake is cooked through.

5. Cover the top with foil so that the cake does not become too dark on top. Remove the cooked cake from
   the oven and pierce some holes with the cake tester.

6. Carefully pour the brandy, rum or amaretto over the
   hot cake. Let the cake cool down completely and
   remove from the cake tin. Wrap tightly in foil. Let it rest
   for 10 days in an airtight container, brushing with more
   brandy every few days until serving.

Let's have a braai

Sweet & Sour Chicken and Mushroom Braai Pie

INGREDIENTS

1 tablespoon olive oil
1 box Fry's chicken-style strips, cut into smaller cubes
1 teaspoon sea salt
1 teaspoon lemon pepper
1 tablespoon olive oil
½ red onion, chopped
½ teaspoon minced garlic
½ green pepper, seeded and finely chopped
1 punnet mushrooms, finely sliced
1 tablespoon chopped coriander
½ can (440 g) crushed pineapple, drained
½ cup Hasty Tasty Sweet & Sour sauce
2 x 400 g rolls of puff pastry
2 tablespoons olive oil

INSTRUCTIONS

1. Place a large saucepan on a braai grid over hot flames. Add the olive oil and heat up. When hot, add the chicken-style cubes, salt and lemon pepper. Fry over the flames until crispy. Transfer the cubes from the saucepan to a mixing bowl and set aside.
2. Heat another tablespoon of olive oil in the saucepan. Add the onion and fry until translucent. Add the garlic, green pepper, mushrooms and chopped coriander.
3. Place over the coals and fry. Add a pinch of salt. Remove from the heat. Add the crushed pineapple, chicken-style cubes and sweet-and-sour sauce to the saucepan. Mix the ingredients and return to the heat for the flavours to marry (about 5 minutes).
4. Roll open one of the puff pastries onto a baking tray. Lightly brush the pastry surface with olive oil. Place the baking tray on the grid. Close the grid and flip it over so that the oil-basted surface sticks to the grid. Open the flipped grid and scoop your delicious filling onto the pastry, spreading it evenly. Leave 1 cm of space on all four sides of the pastry.
5. Place the second piece of pastry onto the baking tray and brush with olive oil. Make sure it's the same size as the first piece of pastry (if not, roll it out slightly). Place the second sheet on top of the filling, with the oil-based side facing upwards. Press the sides of the two pastry sheets together to seal the braai pie.
6. Close the grid and braai the pie over a very low heat until golden and crispy on each side. Remove from the coals.
7. To remove the pie from the grid, carefully place the baking tray inside the grid and flip over so that the pie ends up on the tray.
8. Cut in half, lengthwise, and then into 10 blocks (five on each side).

Tasty Tofu Skewers (Sosaties)

These chunky skewers are crazy creamy and satisfyingly sweet. Good friend Charl and I stacked these for a group of my parents' friends one evening when we were in a slight hurry to get something vegan on the braai. Feel free to substitute the vegetables with what you have, but make sure the veggies all need the same cooking time — in other words, only use soft varieties. To enable smart skewering, check that your vegetable bites are the same size. Not making a fire, but still want to give this recipe a go? Marinate the ingredients and prepare them as a stir-fry in the pan. To give the veggies and tofu a crunchy coating, add some cornstarch to the programme.

INGREDIENTS

400 g firm tofu
1 red onion, quartered and seperated
1 green pepper, seeded and cut into bite-sized chunks
1 pineapple, chopped in bite-size chunks
1 punnet (400 g) mushrooms

For the marinade

½ cup coconut cream
2½ tablespoons peach chutney
1 tablespoon soy sauce
1½ tablespoons Dijon mustard
Salt and pepper

INSTRUCTIONS

1. Drain the liquid from the tofu and pat dry. Cut the tofu into bite-sized cubes: 2 cm x 2 cm x 1 cm. Place the tofu cubes on a piece of paper towel, cover with another piece of paper towel and place a heavy object, like a book, on top to drain the tofu. Change the paper towel if you see it becomes very wet.

2. Place the wooden sosatie skewers in a bowl of water (this is to prevent the skewers from burning on the fire). Mix all the marinade ingredients in a mixing bowl.

3. Remove the sosatie skewers and place the vegetables and tofu on them: first, the mushroom (when skewering mushrooms, do so carefully and slowly through the centre of the mushroom stem).

4. Skewer the rest in the following order: red onion chunk; green pepper chunk; tofu block; pineapple chunk; red onion chunk; green pepper chunk; tofu block; pineapple chunk; mushroom. Place the skewers in a casserole dish, making sure they fit in neatly next to each other, and cover with the marinade for 30 minutes.

5. Braai the skewers over hot coals, turning regularly and brushing the marinade over the skewers as they cook. Leave a bit of the marinade for brushing on after the braai.

6. When the vegetables have softened (even lightly charred) and the tofu is golden, remove them from the braai and place on a serving platter.

7. Pour the remaining marinade over the skewers and serve.

Lentil Dhal-stuffed Peppers on the Coals

INGREDIENTS

1 tablespoon olive oil

1 red onion, finely chopped

2 cloves garlic, minced

1 thumb fresh ginger, grated

½ teaspoon cajun spice

½ teaspoon chilli and garlic seasoning

1 teaspoon paprika

½ teaspoon peri-peri spice

3 tomatoes, chopped

½ cup tomato sauce (I use All Gold)

1 cup broccoli, chopped

3 stalks celery, sliced

1 can (400 ml) coconut milk

1 cup cooked lentils

Pinch of salt and pepper, to taste

4 peppers (any colour), lid cut off and seeded; keep the lids

INSTRUCTIONS

1. Place a saucepan on a grid over medium coals. Add the olive oil to the saucepan and heat up. Once hot, add the onion and fry until translucent. Add the garlic and ginger, frying them with the onion. Add all the spices and coat the ingredients in the spices.

2. Now add the tomatoes, tomato sauce, broccoli, celery, coconut milk and lentils. Mix well to combine. Cover the saucepan and let everything simmer until the flavours marinate and the liquid evaporates.

3. Taste the mix; add salt and pepper if you need it. Scoop the filling into the seeded peppers and close the pepper lids. Place each pepper in a piece of oil-brushed foil — shiny side facing inwards. Carefully wrap the pepper, like you would a sandwich. Place on the grid to cook over low-to-medium heat, until the pepper is soft but still holding its shape. Carefully open the foil package — the steam is really hot — and serve.

Wrap Focaccias over the Coals

INGREDIENTS

2 wraps (gluten-free, whole-wheat or normal)

2 tablespoons olive oil

½ white onion, very finely chopped

8 peppadews, very finely chopped

½ punnet mushrooms, sliced

2 tablespoons fresh parsley, finely chopped

1 clove garlic, crushed / ¾ teaspoon preserved garlic

Grind of sea salt and lemon pepper

1 tablespoon margarine

TIP

Get creative with your ingredients — play with diverse vegetables such as mushrooms, peppers and caramelised onions or add assorted herbs and spices. You can also add grated vegan cheese.

INSTRUCTIONS

1. Brush the wraps with olive oil on both sides. Evenly spread the ingredients over the wraps. Place on a grid over low-heat coals. Cook until the wraps are crispy and start to darken. Remove from the heat, cut into slices and serve as a snack.

Cherry-Berry Yoghurt Puddings

This recipe is quick to whip up if you pre-make the condensed milk and keep it in the fridge. It is a sweet, yet satisfyingly refreshing dessert on those scorching summer days.

INGREDIENTS

For the condensed milk

1 can (400 ml) coconut cream
75 g white sugar

1 packets Simply Delish Zero Cherry or Raspberry Jelly
1 cup cold water
1 cup boiling hot water
125 g cherry / mixed-berry soya yoghurt (available from Woolworths or Urban Vegan SA)

INSTRUCTIONS

1. Make the condensed milk: Place the coconut cream and sugar in a big pot. Bring to the boil, whisking continuously until you've dissolved all the sugar. Be careful; as soon as the mixture starts to boil, it can cook over quickly. If this happens, lift the pot off the heat for a few seconds. As soon as the coconut mixture reaches a rapid boiling stage, reduce the heat and simmer the mixture over a low heat.

2. Continue to simmer for 30 to 45 minutes, stirring occasionally to prevent sugar crystals and the bottom from burning. Do not scrape down the sides. Cook until the mixture reduces its quantity by half (it will become exactly 1 cup) and reaches a thick and sticky consistency. It will look like condensed milk. Remove from the heat and pour into a glass jar.

3. Give the jar another good stir. Place in the fridge to cool (do not put on the lid until cool). Empty the jelly contents into a mixing bowl. Add 1 cup of cold water; whisk until the content is dissolved. Add 1 cup of boiling hot water. Whisk again. Let it set slightly at room temperature.

4. Place the jelly into a food processor. Add ½ cup cooled condensed milk and the soya yoghurt. Process until well combined and smooth. Scoop the filling into glass dessert bowls.

5. Refrigerate for 1 hour. Serve with berry sauce and berry ice cream.

It's early evening

Post-workout Protein Bowl

INGREDIENTS

For the dressing

1 can (400 g) chickpeas, drained

3 tablespoons tahini

1 garlic clove, left whole

1 teaspoon ground cumin

Juice of 1 lemon (about ¼ cup)

¾ cup water

Salt and pepper, to taste

1 cup brown rice

Pinch of salt

4 cups water

1 teaspoon Robertsons Spice for Rice

Oil, for frying

1 onion, finely chopped

1 clove garlic, minced

1 teaspoon ground cumin

1 teaspoon mustard powder

1 can (285 g) sliced mushrooms in brine, drained

Salt and pepper, to taste

3 cups spinach (baby spinach or Swiss chard)

1 teaspoon fresh lemon juice

1 can (400 g) lentils in brine, drained and rinsed

INSTRUCTIONS

1. Make the dressing: Place all the ingredients in a blender and blend until creamy yet runny. If the mixture is too thick, add more water. Set aside.

2. Cook the rice: Rinse the rice until the water runs clean. Add the rice, a pinch of salt and 2 cups of water to a pot and bring to the boil. Cover and cook the rice for 10 minutes over medium heat. Stir often to prevent the rice from burning. Add a third cup of water and cook for another 5 minutes. Add the final cup of water along with 1 teaspoon of Spice for Rice and cook until all the water is absorbed. Drain the rice and set aside.

3. While the rice cooks, make the mushroom mix: Add a drop of oil to a non-stick pan and turn the heat to high. Add the onion and fry until translucent (add a drop of water if the onion starts to brown). Add the garlic and fry until fragrant. Add the cumin and mustard powder and coat the mixture. Add the mushrooms, with a pinch of salt and pepper. Fry until the mushrooms start to brown. Remove from the heat and transfer the mushrooms to a separate bowl.

4. Using the same pan, add ¼ cup of water and bring to a simmer. Add the baby spinach and cook until it becomes bright green and slightly wilted. Add a grind of salt and pepper and the lemon juice. Mix through and remove the spinach from the heat.

5. Mix the drained lentils, cooked rice and mushroom mixture.

6. Serve the rice, lentil and mushroom mixture with a side of spinach and a good drizzle of the dressing.

Brent Meersman's Exceptional Smoothie

Use it as a base for a protein smoothie after gym.
It can also be served as dessert.

INGREDIENTS

Fruit of choice: A cup of mixed frozen raspberries, blueberries and black berries. Straight out of the freezer, they chill down the dessert. Banana and mango also work well as a base

Soya or almond milk, or vegan yoghurt (enough to cover the fruit)

Juice of ½ lime

1 tablespoon peanut butter or another nut butter

1-cm piece of ginger root (chopped)

1 tablespoon maple syrup or agave syrup

Spice (optional): vanilla or saffron (especially if using banana as a base)

1 teaspoon wheat germ

INSTRUCTIONS

1. Blend all the ingredients in a liquidiser. Serve as a dessert in a glass with some fresh berries or slices of banana.
2. Garnish with a teaspoon of wheat germ.

TIP

For a gym protein mix, add 1 tablespoon pea-protein isolate and 1 tablespoon soya protein. You can also add dark-chocolate powder.

Green Goddess Buddha Bowl

INGREDIENTS

1 cup quinoa, cooked

4 teaspoons dairy-free basil pesto

¼ teaspoon salt

1 head broccoli, washed and cut into florets

2 tablespoons lemon juice

½ teaspoon paprika

1 teaspoon olive oil

1 clove garlic, peeled and minced

6 medium zucchinis, spiralised / grated

¼ teaspoon coarse salt

1 cup frozen edamame beans or peas

2 cups baby spinach, washed and dried

1 avocado, pitted and sliced

1 tablespoon basil pesto (see page 56)

1 spring onion, sliced

INSTRUCTIONS

1. Mix the cooked quinoa with the basil pesto and set aside. Heat a pot of water on the stove, add the salt and cook the broccoli until bright green and slightly soft. Drain the broccoli in a colander; add the lemon juice and paprika. Work through with your hands. Leave it in the colander.

2. Add the olive oil to a pan and heat. Add the garlic and fry until fragrant. Add the zucchini spirals and fry quickly until bright green and soft. Set aside.

3. Heat a small pot of water on the stove and add the salt and the edamame beans — cook until the skins pop open and the beans burst out. Drain the beans and dunk in a mixing bowl of ice water. Remove the beans from the skins. Dry slightly and rub with coarse sea salt.

4. Assemble the bowl: Add 1 cup of baby spinach to the bottom of a bowl. Place ½ cup of the cooked quinoa in a ramekin and unmould in the middle of the bowl to create a beautiful heap.

5. Divide the broccoli, zucchini spaghetti and edamame beans between the two bowls, creating a heap of each around the quinoa. Add half the avocado plus a dollop of basil pesto to each bowl. Garnish with spring onion.

Curry pasta salad

INGREDIENTS

For the pasta

½ packet egg-free pasta

1 onion, diced

1 pepper, diced

1 cup raisins

For the sauce

1 cup sunflower oil

½ cup white-wine vinegar

3½ tablespoons curry powder

½ cup tomato sauce

½ cup sugar

3 drops Tabasco sauce (optional)

Salt and pepper, to taste

INSTRUCTIONS

1. Cook the pasta according to the packet instructions. Strain and set aside to cool.
2. Mix all the sauce ingredients in a big bowl.
3. Add the cold pasta to the sauce and mix. Add the onion, pepper and raisins to the pasta and mix.
4. Place in the fridge for an hour to cool.
5. Serve cold.

Italian Tomato Zoodle Salad

This is a simple side dish, but it sure leaves an impression. To create the wow factor, we focus on variety, flavour and effect. We'll use different types of baby tomatoes to build our tower, including cherry, yellow, rosa and green tomatoes. Salting the tomatoes and complementing them with olives and capers will bring out the flavour. The infused dressing evokes warmth and the basil adds freshness.

INGREDIENTS

½ cup pine nuts
350 g baby tomatoes, varied (such as rosa, Tigerella, bella, cherry, Rosallini)
Sea salt and ground black pepper
1 teaspoon dried origanum
6 big zucchinis
2 cloves garlic, minced
8 pitted green olives, pitted and sliced in half
8 pitted Kalamata olives, pitted and sliced in half
6 capers
¼ cup fresh basil, chopped
Fresh basil, for garnish

Dressing

Balsamic vinegar
Olive oil
1 clove garlic, minced
1 red chilli, seeded and finely chopped

INSTRUCTIONS

1. Dry-roast the pine nuts in a hot pan until lightly browned. Set aside.
2. Cut the baby tomatoes into different sizes — sliced, halved and quartered according to their size. Put the sliced tomatoes into a colander and season with a grind of sea salt and dried origanum. Toss the tomatoes and let them sit in the colander for 15 minutes. Discard any juice that seeps out of them.
3. Make the dressing: Mix 1 part vinegar to 3 parts olive oil along with the minced garlic and chopped chilli. Set aside.
4. Once you've completed the dressing, spiralise or grate the zucchinis into noodles (you can also buy already spiralised zoodles).
5. Heat 1 tablespoon coconut oil in a pan and add the minced garlic cloves. Brown lightly. Add the zoodles and season with salt and pepper. Cook until the zoodles soften slightly. Take the zoodles off the heat.
6. Now add the tomatoes, olives, capers and chopped basil to the pan and mix (keep some tomatoes aside to place at the top of the dish). Use tongs to tower the mixture in the centre of a plate.
7. Top with toasted pine nuts and extra tomatoes. Garnish with fresh basil leaves. Serve with a side dressing.

Mac & Cheese Bake

Every household has its own mac & cheese recipe. This one is a bit unconventional — it is a healthy twist on the traditional, yet still as creamy and cheesy. Using tofu in the cheese sauce and Thick Cut Chunky Strips from The Fry Family Food Co range also makes this recipe high in protein. Alternatively, you can also use 4 Fry's Asian-Spiced Burgers, and swop the tofu with a small can of coconut cream.

INGREDIENTS

1 box Fry's Thick Cut Chunky Strips, defrosted

2 tablespoons soya sauce

250 g whole-wheat macaroni

1 tablespoon olive oil (to add to the water so the macaroni doesn't stick)

1 cup firm tofu, drained

1½ cups almond milk, unsweetened

1 cup vegetable stock

½ cup nutritional yeast

2 tablespoons cornstarch

2 tablespoons lemon juice

1 teaspoon Dijon mustard

1 clove garlic

1 teaspoon onion powder (optional)

½ teaspoon turmeric

Salt and pepper, to taste

2 tablespoons breadcrumbs (optional)

INSTRUCTIONS

1. Cut the Fry's Thick Cut Chunky Strips into small cubes and let them marinate in the soya sauce. Boil a pot of water, add a dash of olive oil and cook the macaroni until it is al dente.

2. While the macaroni is cooking, add all the other ingredients (except the breadcrumbs) to a blender and blend until frothy. Set aside.

3. Transfer the marinated Fry's chunky strips to a pan and cook over a medium heat. Remove from the heat and set aside.

4. Preheat the oven to 190°C. Spray a baking dish with cooking spray and set aside.

5. Drain the cooked macaroni, rinse with water, and return it to the pot. Add the Fry's cubes and sauce mixture to the pot, and heat it up over a low heat. Mix the ingredients well. (Don't keep it on the heat for long, just heat it up slightly.)

6. Transfer the mixture to the prepared baking dish, sprinkle with the breadcrumbs, and bake until the crumbs are nicely browned (about 25 minutes).

7. Serve hot.

Spaghetti Cups

This recipe is just as good without the soya mince.

INGREDIENTS

½ packet spaghetti
2 red peppers, seeded and cut into chunks
2 cloves garlic, halved
3 tablespoons tomato paste
Salt and pepper
6 dates, pitted and cut in half
1¼ cups tomato passata sauce
2 onions, chopped
2 cloves garlic, minced
2 teaspoon dried origanum
1 teaspoon paprika
½ teaspoon ground cumin
1 cup grated vegan meltable cheese (Violife for Pizza)

INSTRUCTIONS

1. Cook the spaghetti according to the packet instructions. Drain and set aside.
2. Preheat the oven to 200°C.
3. Make the tomato sauce: Place the red peppers and garlic on a baking sheet and drizzle with olive oil. Roast for 30 minutes or until the peppers are charred. Remove the peppers and garlic from the oven and place in a blender with the tomato paste, salt and pepper, dates and passata. Blend until smooth. (You can store this in the fridge and use as an everyday tomato sauce.)
4. Fry the onions in olive oil until translucent. Add the minced garlic, origanum, paprika and cumin. Mix to cover. Return the mixture to the pan with the onions and spices and mix to combine. Set aside.
5. Turn down the oven to 180°C. Spray a 12-hole muffin pan with cooking spray.
6. Mix the spaghetti and sauce together. Add ¾ of the cheese and stir through. Divide between the 12 muffin cups. Sprinkle the remaining cheese over and bake for 20 to 30 minutes.
7. Scoop out of the muffin pan and serve hot.

TIP
For a sweeter sauce, use more dates.

Hot & Spicy Vegan 'Chicken' Burgers

This dish also made its claim to fame on national television. One afternoon, I showed *Afternoon Express* viewers how to tart up an already spicy chicken-style burger with a delicious red-pepper hummus. We used the Quorn Vegan Hot & Spicy Burgers — they have chilli in the crumbs — and added the finishing touch with a splodge of creamy guacamole. The hummus is also ideal as a dip for crudités, or as a base in wraps.

INGREDIENTS

1 pack Quorn Vegan Hot & Spicy Burgers
4 hamburger rolls
Fresh lettuce / mixed dark leafy greens

For the red-pepper hummus

2 cloves garlic, sliced in half
2 red peppers, seeded and cut in quarters
Olive oil
Grind of sea salt and black pepper
1 can (400 g) chickpeas, drained
2 tablespoons tahini
3 tablespoons lemon juice
1 teaspoon paprika
¼ teaspoon cayenne pepper

For the guacamole

2 ripe Hass avocados (these are the creamiest), pitted
½ cup red onion, chopped
1 tomato, chopped
2 tablespoons fresh coriander, minced
1 tablespoon lemon juice
½ teaspoon chilli flakes
Salt and pepper

INSTRUCTIONS

1. Preheat the oven to 200˚C (grill). Place the garlic halves and red-pepper quarters in an oven-proof dish. Drizzle and rub with olive oil and a grind of salt, and place in the oven. Roast for about 20 minutes, until the red peppers are soft and start to blacken on the sides.
2. Remove the red peppers and garlic halves, turn down the heat to 180˚C and, in the same dish, bake the Quorn patties, turning them once halfway through the baking time.
3. Continue with the red-pepper hummus: Place all the ingredients in a food processor, along with the roasted red-pepper quarters and garlic halves, and blend until smooth. Set aside.
4. Make the guacamole: Mash the avocados, leaving a few chunky pieces in the mash. Add the chopped red onion, tomatoes, coriander, lemon juice, chilli flakes, plus a grind of salt and pepper, and mix through.
5. Cut the hamburger rolls in half and toast them in a toaster, sandwich press or in the oven. Be careful not to burn them.
6. Build your burger: Remove the Quorn patties from the oven. Spread a thick layer of hummus on the sides of the toasted rolls. Place the lettuce on the bottom half of the rolls, stack the Quorn patty on the lettuce, add a dollop of chunky guacamole, and close the burger. Serve with crispy sweet-potato fries.

Roxy Louw's Vegan Mediterranean Chickpea Burgers

Roxy, surfer, model and actress, is the founder of GreenLeaf Vitality and is a yoga instructor.

INGREDIENTS

4 cloves garlic, minced
2 cans (400 g each) chickpeas
Zest and juice of 2 lemons
3 cups baby spinach, chopped
6 to 8 sundried tomatoes, covered in olive oil
½ cup ground oats
2 tablespoons flaxseed powder, mixed with
 3 tablespoons water
¼ cup + 2 tablespoons almond or coconut flour
1 tablespoon nutritional yeast (optional)

INSTRUCTIONS

1. Fry the garlic in 1 tablespoon of the oil used to coat the sundried tomatoes. Place 1 cup of the drained and rinsed chickpeas into a large bowl and the rest in a food processor. Zest both of the lemons into the bowl with the chickpeas. Squeeze the juice of 1 lemon into the food processor with the other half of the chickpeas. Pulse until they are soft, but not puréed — about 20 seconds. Transfer to the large bowl.

2. Blend the spinach in the food processor and transfer to the bowl. Drain the sundried tomatoes, reserving the excess oil to cook the burgers; place them into the food processor and blend. Add the sundried-tomato mixture to the large bowl, along with the sautéed garlic, nutritional yeast, the oats and flax.

3. Squeeze in the juice of the last lemon; add ¼ cup flour and mix again. Add 2 tablespoons of flour while continuing to stir, until it is firm enough to handle. Add more flour as you need it. Line a baking sheet with parchment paper and set aside.

4. Roll out patties with your hands. Refrigerate them for 30 minutes.

5. Once you're ready to cook, warm the oil from the sundried tomatoes in a pan over a medium heat and cook the burgers for 5 minutes, until golden-brown, or deep-fry.

6. Store for up to four days in the fridge or freeze for later use.

Crispy Baked Tofu

INGREDIENTS

1 block firm tofu
3 tablespoons tamari / soya sauce (tamari has more flavour)
1 tablespoon olive oil
1 tablespoon cornstarch
1 teaspoon smoked paprika
1 teaspoon chilli powder / a drop of hot sauce
Cooking spray

INSTRUCTIONS

1. Preheat the oven to 180°C.
2. Drain the tofu and cut it into 1-cm thick strips. Place the tofu strips on a piece of kitchen paper towel, cover with another piece of towel and place a heavy book on top to drain the excess water.
3. Mix the soya sauce and olive oil in a mixing bowl. Add the drained tofu strips and mix to cover all the strips. Add the cornstarch, smoked paprika, chilli powder or hot sauce and mix well to combine.
4. Spray an oven-proof dish with cooking spray and place the tofu strips in the dish. Bake for 20 minutes, turning the tofu after 10 minutes in. Remove the strips and let them cool.
5. Serve with stir-fry veggies, as part of a breakfast fry-up, on a hamburger roll or in a wrap.

Baked Lentil Falafels in Pita Halves

INGREDIENTS
B-Well Canola Cooking Spray

For the falafels
2 cups cooked lentils
½ cup fresh coriander leaves
½ cup fresh parsley leaves
3 scallions (small sweet onions), chopped
2 tablespoons olive oil
3 cloves garlic
2 tablespoons lemon juice
1 tablespoon tahini
½ teaspoon salt
2 teaspoons ground cumin
2 teaspoons ground coriander
½ green chilli, seeded
2 teaspoons baking powder
2 tablespoons all-purpose flour (or a gluten-free flour
   if needed)

For the pita breads
4 vegan pita-bread halves
8 tablespoons hummus (see page 52)
1 cup shredded red cabbage
½ cup cucumber, chopped
½ cup tomatoes, chopped
8 tablespoons tangy tahini dressing
1 tablespoon spring onion, chives or green chilli (optional)

INSTRUCTIONS
1. Preheat the oven to 180°C. Spray an oven-proof dish
   with cooking spray.
2. Make the falafels: Add all the ingredients except the
   flour and baking powder to a blender and mix until well
   combined, but not mushy. Transfer the mixture to a
   mixing bowl. Add the baking powder and first tablespoon of flour, and mix through. Add the second tablespoon of flour and mix again. Use a teaspoon to scoop
   up a dollop of the falafel mixture into your hands.
3. Roll the mixture into balls and place in the prepared
   oven-proof dish. Brush the falafel balls with olive oil
   and bake in the oven for 20 minutes. Turn the falafels
   halfway through baking time (careful, at this stage they
   are fragile). Brush again with olive oil.
4. Assemble the pita breads: Cut open the pita breads
   and spread 2 tablespoons of hummus on the insides of
   each. Add the shredded cabbage, chopped cucumber
   and tomatoes. Add 3 falafel balls per pita bread and
   drizzle with the tangy tahini dressing. Sprinkle with
   spring onion, chives and fresh chilli.

TIP
To help better set the mixture, place the falafel balls in
the fridge overnight before baking. You can also serve
the falafels in wraps or in salads.

'Cheesy' Nachos

Who doesn't love digging into a big plate of crunchy Mexican nachos? The first lunch I enjoyed when I went vegan while studying, was nachos at Cubaña Latino Café and Cigar Lounge in Sea Point, Cape Town. Of course, back then, there were no vegan cheese sauces or sour cream so I had to settle for dry chips with guacamole. Today, I can enjoy them with all the trimmings. These nachos are perfect for lunch or dinner and entertaining friends and family. Best of all, they are healthy. If you're gluten-free, substitute the cheese sauce with a non-flour version.

INGREDIENTS

For the sour cream

1 cup raw cashews, soaked
¼ cup sunflower seeds, soaked
¼ cup lemon juice
1 tablespoon apple-cider vinegar
1 cup water
½ teaspoon salt

For the smashed beans

1 tablespoon olive oil
1 onion, finely chopped
1 clove garlic, minced
1 teaspoon paprika
1 teaspoon ground cumin
½ teaspoon ground coriander
¼ teaspoon cayenne pepper
1 can (400 g) black beans in brine, drained and rinsed
1 can (400 g) chopped tomatoes and onion mix
1 tablespoon tomato paste
1 teaspoon Chipotle Tabasco (smoked Tabasco)
Squeeze of lemon juice

For the cheese sauce

½ cup cake-wheat flour (all-purpose flour), sifted
3 cups unsweetened soya milk
¾ cup nutritional yeast
1 teaspoon salt
1 teaspoon garlic powder
Sprinkle of turmeric (just for colour)
A grind or two of black pepper

For the guacamole

2 avocados, pitted
1 to 2 tablespoons lemon juice
¼ teaspoon cayenne pepper
Salt and pepper

1 packet (250 g) nacho chips
2 chillis, seeded and sliced or 1 tablespoon
   chilli flakes (optional)

Continue on page 142

'Cheesy' Nachos

INSTRUCTIONS

1. Make the sour cream: Drain the cashews and sunflower seeds. Place in the blender along with the lemon juice, apple-cider vinegar, water and salt. Blend until smooth. Set aside.

2. Make the smashed beans: Heat the olive oil in a pan over a high heat. Turn heat down to low, add the onion and fry until translucent. Add the garlic and fry until browned slightly. Add all the spices and mix through the onion and garlic. Add the drained beans and mix through. Smash some of the beans using a potato smasher. Add the tomato and onion mix, the tomato paste and Chipotle Tabasco. Simmer over a low heat until the water from the tomato and onion mix has evaporated. Take off the heat and adjust the seasoning according to taste. Mix through a squeeze of lemon juice. Set aside.

3. Make the 'cheese' sauce: Sift the flour into the cold soya milk. Add the nutritional yeast, salt and garlic powder. Whisk until combined. Transfer to a pot and cook over a low heat. Whisk continuously until thick and lump-free. Transfer the sauce to a food processor or blender and mix until smooth and velvety.

4. Make the guacamole: Mash the avocados with a fork until chunky. Add the lemon juice, cayenne pepper, salt and pepper and mash again. Set aside.

5. Assemble the nachos: Lay out four plates and scatter nacho chips evenly between the plates. Drench the nachos with cheese sauce. Divide the smashed beans between the plates by adding a big scoop of the mixture in the middle of the nachos. Add a dollop of guacamole on top of the beans. Add small dollops of sour cream on top of the nachos. Sprinkle with fresh chilli flakes.

Mushroom & Yellow Lentil Dhal

INGREDIENTS

500 g split dhal (yellow lentils)
¼ teaspoon turmeric powder
Pinch of salt
1 punnet mushrooms, sliced
4 tablespoons coconut oil
1 medium-sized onion, chopped
4 cloves garlic, peeled and minced
2 level tablespoons curry powder
¼ teaspoon ground cumin
¼ teaspoon ground coriander
1 stem curry leaves
1 tomato, finely chopped
Salt, to taste
Fresh coriander, for garnish

INSTRUCTIONS

1. Rinse the lentils until the water runs clear. Place the lentils in a pot and cover with water. Add the turmeric powder and salt. Boil until the lentils start softening. Drain and set aside.
2. In a non-stick pan, fry the mushrooms in 1 tablespoon of coconut oil until brown. Remove from the pan.
3. In the same pan, add the remaining coconut oil and fry the onion until translucent, add the garlic and fry further until brown. Add the curry powder, cumin, coriander, curry leaves and tomato. Allow the tomato to cook through; add the fried mushrooms and drained lentils. Allow it to simmer until it reaches a thick consistency.
4. Season to taste and garnish with coriander. Serve with rice or rotis.

Let's dine and wine

Sweet Butternut Soup

No winter is complete without a traditional South African butternut soup. In our home, it's a staple that we whip up in bulk as soon as the cold creeps in. This recipe is super sweet and creamy, yet cream-less *nogal*, and can be frozen in serving-size portions for Manic Mondays. Served with crunchy pumpkin seeds and crisp ciabatta, this soup makes for a scrumptious starter or a decadent dinner.

INGREDIENTS

3 tablespoons water

2 onions, peeled and finely chopped

1 clove garlic, minced

1 teaspoon fresh ginger, grated

1 kg butternut, peeled, seeded and chopped into pieces (the smaller pieces will cook faster)

4 cups vegetable stock

1 teaspoon nutmeg

½ teaspoon ground cumin

½ teaspoon ground cinnamon

½ teaspoon ground ginger

¼ cup pumpkin seeds

½ cup coconut milk, plus extra for drizzling

INSTRUCTIONS

1. Add the water and onions to a pot and cook over a low heat until translucent. Add the garlic and ginger and mix with the onions. Add the butternut pieces and coat with the onions, garlic and ginger. Add the vegetable stock and spices. The liquid should cover the butternut. Bring to the boil with the lid on and cook until the butternut is super-soft (about 20 minutes).

2. Dry-roast the pumpkins seeds in a pan (no oil) until they swell up.

3. Add the coconut milk to the soup mixture and transfer the content to a blender. Or use a hand blender and blend until smooth. (Be careful, the content is hot. Start on the lowest-possible blender setting.)

4. Transfer to four bowls and garnish with a drizzle of coconut milk and the crunchy pumpkin seeds.

Thai Red-curry Noodle Soup

Pulse pastas are trending on the foodie scene. Not only are they gluten-, egg- and wheat-free, they're also full of protein, making this an easy way to consume your three-a-day. As you will tell by this book, I adore cooking with pasta. Using red lentil or chickpea fusilli is a terrific, guilt-free way of indulging in my favourite food. This curry creation is a hybrid between Italian and Thai cuisine. Red-curry paste is usually really spicy, so I would suggest making your own if you prefer mellow and mild flavour.

INGREDIENTS

2 tablespoons olive oil
1 large onion, finely chopped
2 teaspoons fresh ginger, grated
2 cloves garlic, minced
3 tablespoons red-curry paste
4 cups vegetable stock
125 g Happy Earth People Red Lentil Pasta (or use whole-wheat pasta)
1 punnet mushrooms, sliced
2 cups zucchini, sliced
½ head broccoli, chopped into bite-sized pieces
1 red pepper, seeded, cored and sliced
1 can (400 ml) coconut milk
4 to 5 dried makrut lime leaves
¼ cup chopped fresh coriander
Juice of ½ lemon
Salt and freshly ground black pepper, to taste

INSTRUCTIONS

1. In a non-stick pot or wok, heat the oil over a high heat. Add the chopped onion and lower the heat. Cook the onion until translucent. Add the ginger and garlic and mix through. Add the curry paste and coat the mixture.

2. Pour in the vegetable stock and bring to the boil. Add the red-lentil pasta and cook for 3 minutes. Add the rest of the vegetables, the coconut milk and makrut lime leaves and cook for another 5 minutes until the vegetables are cooked, but still crunchy. Stir in the chopped coriander and lemon juice and season with salt and pepper.

3. Remove the makrut lime leaves and serve with coriander scattered on top.

Couscous Salad with Caramelised Brussels Sprouts & Cranberry Glaze

INGREDIENTS

1 cup cooked couscous

1 cup vegetable stock, to cook couscous

½ packet Brussels sprouts, washed, trimmed and halved

2 cloves garlic, halved

1 tablespoon olive oil, for roasting

Salt and pepper

1 cup cranberry juice

2 tablespoons maple syrup

1 tablespoon pine nuts

1 cup washed and dried baby spinach

2 tablespoons dried cranberries

INSTRUCTIONS

1. Preheat the oven to 150°C.
2. Make the couscous: Add the couscous and vegetable stock to a bowl, making sure you've covered all the grains in liquid. Cover for 15 to 20 minutes until all the water is absorbed. Scrape the couscous with a fork until fluffy. Set aside.
3. Add the Brussels sprouts and garlic to an oven-proof dish and drizzle with olive oil; sprinkle with salt and pepper. Roast for 30 minutes, tossing the Brussels sprouts occasionally, until they turn brown and crispy on the outside and tender on the inside.
4. While the Brussels sprouts are roasting, make the cranberry glaze: Add the cranberry juice and maple syrup to a saucepan. Let them simmer for 15 minutes over a low heat, until the liquid transforms into a syrup-like consistency.
5. Add the pine nuts to a clean saucepan and dry-roast until they become fragrant and slightly brown. Set aside to cool.
6. Mix the baby spinach leaves with the couscous and cranberries; transfer the salad to a salad bowl. Top the salad with a heap of roasted Brussels sprouts. Pour the cranberry glaze over the sprouts and sprinkle with the roasted pine nuts.

Patrick Knight's Carrot Lox (Vegan 'Smoked Salmon')

Patrick is a vegan chef and partner in Green & Vegan Pop-up Dining. Since they have been doing their vegan pop-up dining, featuring vegan sushi, they improved this recipe a lot. Here's the updated recipe.

INGREDIENTS

6 large carrots, washed and scrubbed with
  ends removed
½ sheet nori
2 tablespoons olive oil
2 tablespoons lemon juice
1 tablespoon smoked salt
1 tablespoon liquid smoke-concentrate

TIP

Liquid smoke comes in various concentrations. Some brands are quite diluted and you'll need more than I've specified in this recipe. If it actually says 'concentrate' on the bottle, you can follow this recipe. Be very hygienic in how you handle the carrots, otherwise the final product won't keep long. I use gloves when massaging the marinade, plus tongs or clean utensils to move shavings from bowl to dehydrator.

INSTRUCTIONS

1. Cut the carrots in half lengthwise. Using a mandoline, make as many carrot shavings as you can. I make some on the medium thickness and some thinner.

2. Bring a pot of water on the stove to the boil. Drop the carrot shavings into the water and cook for 6 to 8 minutes. You want the carrots to soften slightly, but not to cook too much. Drain immediately. Put the nori sheet at the bottom of a bowl or flat dish.

3. Being careful not to break the carrot shavings, spread them out on top of the nori. In a small bowl, make a marinade with the olive oil, lemon juice, smoked salt and liquid smoke. Mix well and pour over the carrots, and try to get all shavings coated.

4. Let the carrots marinate for several hours. You want to get this going while the carrots are still warm, so they soak up the flavours. Wearing a glove, gently massage the marinade into the carrot shavings to ensure you coat everything well. After completing this, cold-smoke the shavings for that little extra smokiness.

5. Use whatever smoking method you have, or even skip this step.

6. Lastly, spread the shavings out on a dehydrator sheet and dry for about 45 minutes to one hour. Don't dry them too long as the carrots will shrivel up.

Aubergines, Peppers & Green Apples Curry

INGREDIENTS

2 to 3 teaspoons coconut oil

1 medium-sized onion, chopped

2 large cloves garlic, peeled and minced

2 tablespoons curry powder

½ teaspoon turmeric powder

½ teaspoon ground cumin

½ teaspoon ground coriander

5 bay leaves

1 can (410 g) of Miami tomato, basil, garlic and origanum

4 large tomatoes, finely chopped

1 large aubergine, cut into bite-sized pieces (you can also use 1 punnet of button mushrooms, halved)

1 green pepper, seeded, pitted and cut into strips, lengthwise

1 green apple, cored and cut into bite-sized pieces

Salt, to taste

2 tablespoons soy sauce

1 to 2 teaspoons brown sugar (optional, use only if the tomatoes are sour)

2 tablespoons fresh coriander, to garnish

INSTRUCTIONS

1. In a pot, melt the coconut oil and fry the onion until translucent. Add the garlic and fry further until brown.
2. Add the curry powder, turmeric, cumin, coriander and bay leaves and coat the onions and garlic in the spices.
3. Add the tinned tomato mix and chopped tomatoes and mix through. Allow the tomato to simmer over medium heat for about 5 minutes.
4. Add the aubergine, green pepper and apple. Season with salt. Allow to simmer over medium to low heat for about 10 to 15 minutes.
5. When the aubergines, apples and green peppers are soft, add the soy sauce and brown sugar (if using) and mix through.
6. Garnish with fresh coriander and serve with cooked rice, couscous or rotis.

Vegan Butter 'Chicken' with Quorn

I created this dish for the *Afternoon Express* show, when they asked me to whip up a wholesome vegan meal using Quorn Vegan Savoury Pieces (one of four vegan products on the local market). It is a creamy and comforting curry, rich in authentic Indian aromas.

INGREDIENTS

1 box Quorn Vegan Savoury Pieces or Strips, cut into bite-sized cubes

For the marinade

1 can (400 ml) coconut cream
2 teaspoons garam masala spice mix
1 clove garlic, minced
½ teaspoon fresh ginger, grated
Juice of ½ lime or lemon

For the sauce

½ cup raw cashews, soaked overnight in 1 cup of water
1 tablespoon olive or coconut oil
1 small white onion, diced
2 cloves garlic, minced
1 teaspoon fresh ginger, grated
1 tablespoon garam masala spice mix, plus additional to taste
½ teaspoon paprika
1½ teaspoons turmeric
1½ teaspoons ground cumin
6 tomatoes, chopped
1 tablespoon tomato paste
Salt and pepper, to taste
½ teaspoon cayenne pepper
1 tablespoon nutritional yeast
Fresh coriander, to garnish

INSTRUCTIONS

1. Combine all the marinade ingredients in a bowl and add the Quorn cubes. Set aside and let them marinate while you prepare the sauce.
2. Blend the soaked cashews with the water until it becomes a creamy sauce. Scoop out a dollop and keep aside for garnish.
3. Heat the oil in a deep non-stick pot. Add the chopped onion and cook over medium-low heat until translucent. Add the garlic, ginger, garam masala, paprika, turmeric and cumin. Mix until the onions are coated and fragrant. Add the chopped tomatoes, tomato paste, and a pinch of salt to the pan and mix. The tomatoes will release a lot of liquid. Simmer for 30 minutes to an hour, until all excess juices have evaporated. Once you've reduced the mixture to a paste, add it plus the cashews to the blender, and blend until smooth. Add additional water if needed.
4. Return the sauce to the pan and add the Quorn cubes as well as the marinade. Simmer until heated through. Add the cayenne pepper, nutritional yeast, and salt and pepper. Taste and adjust the flavour, adding more garam masala if you need some. Serve hot with basmati rice or naan bread. Garnish with a dollop of cashew cream and fresh coriander.

'Chicken' & Mushroom Pie

I am not a pie-ish kinda gal, but this dish is one I'll devour any day. At first I wanted to use the filling for a different dish (you know, my pie thing), but I gave it an adventurous bash nonetheless — and have adored it ever since. I used Fry's Chicken-style Strips, but you can substitute this with the Quorn Savoury Pieces or thawed chicken-style soya peddled at many Indian restaurants. This recipe also makes for marvellous mini-pies — and it is freezer-friendly. I often find that I have a bit of leftover sauce and filling, which I keep in the fridge to toss with spaghetti when I'm in a hurry.

INGREDIENTS

2 rolls Today Original Puff Pastry
1 box (380 g) Fry's Chicken-style Strips
1 tablespoon olive oil
2 teaspoons chicken spice
1 white onion, chopped
2 cloves garlic, minced
1 teaspoon dried origanum
1 big green pepper, seeded and chopped
2 punnets mushrooms, sliced
1 packet Knorr Thick White Onion Soup
½ cup chickpea flour
½ cup water
800 ml unsweetened soya milk
Salt and pepper

INSTRUCTIONS

1. Preheat the oven to 200°C. Spray an oven-proof pie dish (23 cm) with cooking spray. Roll out 1 roll of puff pastry and press gently into the pie dish. Keep the second roll for the top of the pie. Set aside.
2. Place the defrosted chicken-style strips in the food processor. Pulse the pieces until they're finely chopped.
3. Heat the olive oil in a big (28 cm) non-stick pan. Add the chopped chicken-style pieces with the chicken spice. Fry on a high heat until the pieces are brown and crispy. Pour into a bowl and set aside.
4. In the same pan, add another tablespoon of olive oil and fry the onion until translucent. Add the garlic and origanum and fry for 2 minutes. Add the green pepper and mushrooms. Fry until slightly browned. Add a grind of salt — the salt helps the mushrooms release their water — as well as the onion soup. Cook until all the water has evaporated. Take off the heat and add the chopped chicken-style pieces to the pan.
5. In a bowl, whisk the chickpea flour with the water and set aside. In a deep pot, add 800 ml of the soya milk to the packet of onion soup. Whisk until you've dissolved all the powder. Turn on the heat and bring to a boil, whisking continuously. When the mixture starts to boil, lower the heat and slowly pour the chickpea flour mixture into the sauce.
6. Continue to stir while the mixture is simmering. Once you've combined it well and it starts to thicken, remove from the heat and pour it into the pan along with the mushroom and chicken-style pieces. Scoop the mixture into the dish with pastry until full. Place the second piece of pastry on top and seal by pinching together the dough.
7. Use a fork to press down the sides of the dough and make a border.
8. For decoration, add a pastry cross to the centre of the pie. Brush the pastry with a thin layer of olive oil.
9. Bake for 20 to 30 minutes until the pie is golden-brown. Let it cool slightly and let the filling set, cut in slices and serve with a salad or vegetables.

Rosemary Mushroom Risotto

Who doesn't adore indulging in a big bowl of scrumptious risotto? This deluxe one-pot dish might sound intimidating, but is extremely easy to prepare. It requires exactly 10 ingredients — most of which you'll probably find in your pantry. We have a big rosemary bush growing in our garden, so it's my go-to herb for flavouring mushrooms. But you can use thyme, origanum or parsley instead. You can also substitute the mushrooms with roasted butternut or sweet beetroot.

INGREDIENTS

Oil, for frying
1 small onion, chopped
1 clove garlic, chopped
1 punnet brown mushrooms, sliced
1 to 2 teaspoons Robertsons Mixed Herbs
125 g (¼ packet) Arborio rice
3 cups vegetable stock
2 sprigs fresh rosemary, 1 chopped; 1 whole for garnish
Garlic flakes
Chilli flakes
Ground black pepper to taste

INSTRUCTIONS

1. In a big pan or skillet, heat the olive oil on a medium-to-high temperature (setting 4). Fry the onion until translucent, add the garlic and mushrooms. Stir frequently until the mushrooms and onion start to brown. Add the rice and mixed herbs. Stir well, coating the rice in the pan juices. Turn down the temperature (setting 3).

2. Add enough stock to the pan to cover the rice mixture. Let it simmer over a low heat. Stir continuously (in one direction only) until all the stock is absorbed. Add another big scoop of stock and continue to stir. Repeat until all the stock is used and the rice is creamy and soft (about 20 minutes of cooking).

3. In between scoops, add the chopped rosemary, garlic flakes, chilli flakes and ground pepper to taste. Serve immediately with a sprig of fresh rosemary as garnish.

Pasta Bake with Broccoli, Butternut & Sundried Tomatoes

Another home staple that got its 15 minutes of television fame. I whipped up this pasta bake with broccoli, butternut and sundried tomatoes for a promotion using Clover's unsweetened soya milk. I munch it way too often and make it for dinner parties and potluck clubs, too. Happy Earth People's protein-packed Red Lentil Pasta — instead of regular fusilli pasta — is a marvellous way of infusing nutrition into this dish.

INGREDIENTS

250 g Happy Earth People Red Lentil Pasta
1 head broccoli, washed and chopped
1 packet (500 g) butternut cubes
Olive oil
Salt and pepper
¾ cup all-purpose flour, sifted
3 cups unsweetened soya milk
4 tablespoons sundried tomato oil (from the packet)
6 to 8 Woolworths sundried tomatoes in oil, chopped
1 cup breadcrumbs
Sriracha sauce (or another hot sauce)
Fresh parsley, to garnish

INSTRUCTIONS

1. Cook the pasta according to the packet instructions, drain and set aside. Place the broccoli and butternut in an oven-proof dish. Sprinkle with olive oil, salt and pepper and roast for 30 to 40 minutes at 180°C until soft and caramelised.

2. While the veggies are roasting, make the white sauce: Sift the flour into the soya milk and whisk until combined. Transfer to a pot and bring to the boil. Turn down the heat, add the sundried tomatoes' oil and whisk continuously over a very low heat until thick and lump-free. Add salt and pepper to taste. If your white sauce becomes lumpy, transfer it to a food processor or blender and mix until smooth and velvety.

3. Add the pasta, chopped sundried tomatoes and vegetables to the dish. Mix well to evenly spread the ingredients. Pour over the white sauce and mix. Top with an even layer of breadcrumbs and bake for about 30 minutes. Cut into squares and serve with a squirt of Sriracha sauce and fresh parsley.

Rainbow Rolls with Marinated Tofu

This is a favourite I like to create for dinner parties. It is healthy, fresh, modest and beautiful. The prep work is quite a lot, so feel free to tick off some of the steps the day before — like making the marinade and dipping sauce, plus cutting the veggies. You can also replace the tofu with burger patty strips or Fry's Battered Prawn-style Pieces, which will eliminate draining, pressing and marinating the tofu. Or get your guests to roll their own rolls — it is a fun activity that will make your job a little less, and might send them home with a new skill.

INGREDIENTS

For the tofu marinade

6 tablespoons soya sauce
1 tablespoon apple-cider vinegar
1 clove garlic, minced
2 teaspoons fresh ginger, grated
1 tablespoon maple syrup
¼ teaspoon Sriracha sauce
Juice of ½ a lemon, about 2 tablespoons
2 teaspoons brown sugar (optional)

1 block firm tofu
2 carrots, peeled
1 red pepper, pitted
1 yellow pepper, pitted
¼ cucumber
1 avocado, pitted
100 g vermicelli, rice or glass noodles
1 tablespoon sesame oil
16 rice-paper sheets
½ cup fresh coriander or mint leaves
Edible flowers, to garnish

For the peanut satay sauce

3 tablespoons peanut butter, unsalted and
   sugar-free if possible
5 tablespoons soya sauce
2 teaspoons apple-cider vinegar
2 teaspoons maple syrup
1 fresh chilli, seeded and chopped
1 tablespoon fresh coriander, chopped
2 teaspoons fresh ginger, grated
5 to 6 tablespoons water
Juice of ¼ lemon, about 1 tablespoon

Continue on page 168

Rainbow Rolls with Marinated Tofu

INSTRUCTIONS

1. Combine all the tofu marinade ingredients in a mixing bowl and transfer to an elongated container (one that is big enough to ensure all the tofu lies flat). Drain the water from the tofu and pat dry. Cut the tofu into 8 strips and lay them flat on a paper towel. Place another paper towel on top of the tofu slices (I often replace the towels halfway through to drain more water). Place a heavy object on top of the paper towel (a book will do). Or use a cutting board, prepping the next few meal steps on the board itself, and applying strategic pressure.

2. On the cutting board, cut the carrots, red pepper, yellow pepper, cucumber and avocado into thin julienne strips and set aside.

3. Remove the paper towels from the tofu and cut each strip in half (making 16 strips). Place the tofu strips in the marinade, making sure you lather each one in sauce. Set aside while you prep the noodles.

4. Flip the tofu slices halfway through. Boil a kettle of water. Place the rice noodles in a mixing bowl and top with boiling water. Stir through the noodles once they become loose. When the noodles are soft, drain the water and rinse the noodles with cold water to stop them from cooking. Add the sesame oil to the noodles to prevent them from sticking to each other. Set aside.

5. Make the peanut satay sauce by combining all the ingredients in a mixing bowl and whisking until smooth.

6. Assemble your rolls: Fill a big bowl with very warm water (the bowl must be big enough for one round rice-paper sheet to fit comfortably). Hold the top of the rice-paper sheet and dip into the water, submerge for 15 seconds (or until the rice-paper sheet is soft), lift out of the water and place in front of you.

7. Place the cucumber sticks one thumb away from the bottom of the sheet. Place some rice noodles on top (it's okay if they fall off). Place the carrot sticks behind the rice noodles. Place a strip of tofu on top of the rice noodles.

8. Fold the empty-sheet section at the bottom over the filling and tuck under the carrot sticks. Place a few slices of avo, plus red and yellow peppers against the roll. Holding it in place, position 3 coriander leaves, mint leaves or flowers one thumb away from the top of the sheet. Fold in the sheet sides towards the centre — this ensures your second filling does not pop out. Finally, roll the entire roll from the bottom all the way to the top. Seal the edges and place in a container. Repeat to create 16 rolls.

TIP

Cover all the complete rolls with a damp cloth to prevent them from drying out. Want to cut the rolls in half before serving? Wrap them in cling film and cut with a sharp, non-serrated knife. Remove plastic and serve with the peanut satay sauce. You don't have to use the veggies in the order mentioned — have fun and play around with different varieties!

Vegan Chocolate Mousse

INGREDIENTS

1 large ripe avocado, pitted and chopped

2 tablespoons cacao powder

½ cup almond milk

2 tablespoons agave syrup or maple syrup

1 teaspoon natural vanilla extract or essence

INSTRUCTIONS

1. Place all the ingredients in a blender or food processor and purée until smooth (I find it easier to use a hand blender).

TIP

Add more agave to make this mousse a little sweeter.

Aqua 'Fab' Meringues

Whoever thought you could call on chickpea brine — aquafaba — to make deliciously decadent vegan desserts? This recipe works wonders but it represents a delicate balance, so I recommend that you don't substitute or adjust anything. You can decide, however, if you want to make small, bite-sized meringues; bigger, mountain-like desserts or even one big Pavlova.

INGREDIENTS

Brine from 1 can (400 g) chickpeas (keep the chickpeas for another recipe)

½ teaspoon cream of tartar powder (buy a small packet from your local retailer, it's in the baking aisle with the baking powder)

1 cup icing sugar

Optional: Essence of choice to give your meringues a different flavour. I like using Flavour Nation's Bubblegum Flavouring.

INSTRUCTIONS

1. Preheat the oven to 100°C. If you're using a convection oven (with a fan), preheat to 90°C.

2. Line a baking tray with parchment paper or a silicone mat (this mat must be squeaky-clean — if there is an oil residue, the meringues will collapse).

3. In a clean, metal mixing bowl, add the chickpea brine. Using an electric mixer, whip the brine at high speed for 5 to 6 minutes until it has doubled in size and turned white and foamy. Add the cream of tartar powder and whip for another minute on high speed.

4. Turn the electric mixer to a low setting and slowly add the icing sugar, 1 tablespoon at a time. When you've added all the sugar, turn back the mixer to high speed. Continue to whip for approximately 15 minutes until the mixture becomes thick, white and glossy, and forms stiff peaks when you insert a spoon and pull it out. Make sure the peaks are stiff; that means they should not curl over. If they do, whip for another few minutes — don't worry, you can't over-whip meringues.

It's late
at night

Blissful Berry Balls

INGREDIENTS

1 cup almond flour
1 cup desiccated coconut (use ½ for rolling at the end)
2 tablespoons dried cranberries
2 tablespoons dried goji berries
1 cup dates, pitted and soaked in hot water
3 tablespoons water (from the soaked dates)

INSTRUCTIONS

1. Place the almond flour and dessicated coconut in a food processor and pulse until mixed.
2. Add the cranberries and goji berries and process until the berries are broken into little pieces (this might take a bit longer than expected). Add the chewy, soaked dates and 3 tablespoons of date water to the bowl of the processor and mix until a gooey dough forms. Scrape down the sides with a silicone spatula from time to time
3. Wet your fingers and roll dollops of dough into balls (the size of a R5 coin). Roll the balls into the leftover desiccated coconut and place in an airtight container. Keep the balls in the fridge.

Almond & Peanut Butter Date Balls

INGREDIENTS

1 cup dried dates, pitted and soaked in boiling water
3 tablespoons water (from the soaked dates)
½ cup rolled oats
3 tablespoons peanut or almond butter
¼ cup chopped almonds
¼ cup ground almonds
1 tablespoon chia seeds
Another ¼ cup ground almonds, for rolling

INSTRUCTIONS

1. Drain the dates, preserving 3 tablespoons of date water.
2. Place the dates and date water into a food processor and mix until it forms a dough.
3. Add the oats, peanut butter, chopped almonds, ground almonds and chia seeds. Mix until well combined
4. Sprinkle the extra ground almonds on a chopping board for rolling.
5. Scoop a heaped teaspoon of date-ball dough into your hands and roll into a ball. Then roll into the ground almonds. When all 16 balls are rolled, place them on a plate and transfer it to the fridge to set.

Avo Chocolate Truffles

INGREDIENTS

100 g 70% dark chocolate

1 small, ripe avocado, pitted

Pinch of salt, to taste

1 teaspoon vanilla essence / 15 drops Flavour Nation
  choc-mint drops

1 tablespoon cacao powder

1 teaspoon brown sugar / 5 drops of Flavour Nation
Sweetener / Stevia (optional)

Coating

Raw cacao powder, desiccated coconut or ground
  almonds

INSTRUCTIONS

1. Boil a kettle of water for melting the chocolate in a double boiler. Blend the avocado into a smooth consistency. (If you do not have a food processor, you can mash the avocado with a fork.) Prepare the coating ingredients in a bowl. Cut wax paper to fit into a tray or plate.

2. Cooking: Break the chocolate into smaller pieces and melt it in a double boiler over a low heat. Add the salt and vanilla essence or flavouring. Remove from the heat once the chocolate has melted. Add the chocolate and cacao powder to the blender with the avocado. (This is where you'll add the brown sugar, sweetener drops or Stevia if you wanted to make your truffles sweeter.)

3. Blend or mix the chocolate and avocado mix through until you have a smooth, thick, pudding-like consistency. Transfer the food processor bowl into the fridge for about 30 minutes.

4. After 30 minutes, check the consistency — if it is still too soft to handle, put it in the fridge for another 5 to 10 minutes. When the chocolate and avocado mixture is solid enough to manage, scoop up a little bit of the stiffened chocolate with a teaspoon and roll it in your hands into a smooth ball.

5. Transfer the ball to the coating (cacao powder, desiccated coconut or ground almonds) and roll it until it is completely covered. Place the covered ball on a tray or plate.

6. Place the chocolate truffles back in the fridge and keep it chilled until serving time.

Oreo Peanut-Butter Truffles

Not boasting much of a sweet tooth, I wasn't sure if I ought to add this recipe.
Yet, I do like to whip this up for my family and for friends — they gobble them up
within a day. Perhaps you'll love them, too. It makes for a nice post-dinner treat with
coffee, plus a fabulous food gift for friends. I coat the Oreo balls in melted chocolate and desiccated coconut, but you can skip this step and enjoy them as is.

INGREDIENTS

1 pack Oreos
1 tablespoon cacao
½ cup icing sugar
½ cup desiccated coconut
¼ cup melted coconut oil / Olé margarine
3 tablespoons peanut butter
¼ cup golden syrup
2 x 100 g dark chocolate slabs (I use Cadbury
　Bournville Classic Dark Chocolate)
2 teaspoons coconut oil or Olé margarine
1 cup extra desiccated coconut, Hundreds-and-
　thousands or cacao, for rolling

INSTRUCTIONS

1. Place the Oreos in a food processor and mix until they look like breadcrumbs. Mix the Oreos with the cacao, icing sugar and desiccated coconut in a mixing bowl.
2. Place the coconut oil, peanut butter and golden syrup in a different mixing bowl and microwave for 1 minute to melt. Stir to combine the wet ingredients. Mix the wet into the dry ingredients until well combined. Place the bowl of mixture into the fridge for 15 minutes to cool down and set.
3. Using your hands, roll the mixture into little balls, place in a container lined with baking paper and place in the fridge to set again.
4. Melt the chocolate using a double broiler: place a big pot of water on the stove on a high heat. Place a little pot inside the big pot, making sure the pot's brim touches the boiling water. Break the slabs into blocks and place into the small pot, along with the coconut oil.
5. Add a tablespoon of desiccated coconut (or another topping) into a coffee cup. Once the chocolate and coconut oil have melted, place one Oreo ball into the melting chocolate and swirl around to coat. Then place the ball into a cup with desiccated coconut and swirl around to coat. Place the ball in a clean container. Repeat with all the balls. After a few balls, you'll need to top up the desiccated coconut in the cup.
6. Keep the balls in the fridge until you serve them.

Caramel Sauce

INGREDIENTS

1 cup sugar
⅓ cup water
2 teaspoons lemon juice
1 cup coconut cream, at room temperature
1 tablespoon vegan margarine (Cardin)
1 teaspoon vanilla essence

INSTRUCTIONS

1. Add the sugar to a non-stick pot (non-stick is a biggy here). Do not turn on the heat yet. Add the water and lemon juice to the pot, stirring with a wooden spoon or silicone spatula to cover every grain of sugar in liquid. Yes: an uncovered sugar grain can crystallise your whole pot of caramel. Remove the wooden spoon or spatula and rinse well to avoid further crystallising. Finally, turn up the heat to boiling point. Let the sugar mixture boil, but do not stir it. Simply swirl the pot from time to time.

2. Once the water has evaporated and the mixture becomes an amber colour, remove it from the heat. Be careful not to boil it for too long or your caramel will become bitter. Add the coconut cream and margarine (room temperature coconut cream should prevent the mixture from splattering) and stir in quickly using a wooden spoon or spatula. Don't use metal because it quickly transfers heat, which could result in burning hands.

3. Put the pot back on the stove and simmer the mixture over a low heat, stirring continuously until the mixture is smooth. Remove from the heat, add the vanilla essence and stir through. Pour the caramel into a glass container and place in the fridge to cool and thicken.

4. Enjoy it over vegan ice cream, pancakes or flapjacks, other desserts and sweets.

Chocolate Sauce

A simple, sweet chocolate sauce that'll take minutes to nail. You can keep the sauce in the fridge; however, the coconut oil will set. To use at a later stage, simply reheat the sauce in a pot over a low heat before serving.

INGREDIENTS

⅓ cup coconut oil
⅓ cup raw cacao powder
⅓ cup maple syrup
1 teaspoon vanilla essence

INSTRUCTIONS

1. Melt the coconut oil, cacao powder, maple syrup and vanilla essence in a pot over a low heat.
2. Serve immediately on flapjacks or waffles, over banana ice cream or even on the inside of your chocolate-smoothie glasses.

DINING OUT

Even the most enthusiastic vegan foodies can loathe the idea of toiling over the stove. Thankfully, vegan and vegetarian restaurants are beginning to flourish in South Africa. Vegan options on chain-restaurant menus are also blossoming now, making it as easy as pro-life pie for vegans to dine out with friends and family.

Today, we can have our pick of all sorts of cuisines, health food and even junk food — not forgetting the abundance of vegan goods for sale at farmers' markets. Don't see any vegan options on the menu? Ask the waiter to call the chef and see which ingredients they can substitute to suit your needs. I have always found restaurants and chefs very accommodating.

If you want to know more about the restaurants listed below, as well as their menu selections, read reviews on local vegan food blogs and websites, such as Cape Town Vegan, CTVeganista, Happy Cow and Vegan SA.

MY FAVOURITE PURELY VEGAN AND VEGETARIAN RESTAURANTS

GAUTENG

Bella Anima
6 Sunhill Centre, Sunninghill (at Tana Road & Naivasha Road), Johannesburg

Conscious 108
108 Greenway Road, Greenside, Johannesburg

Free Food
Shop 5B Reithmere, cnr Delta Road & Corlett Drive, Birnam, Johannesburg

Fresh Earth
103 Komatie Street, Emmarentia, Gauteng, Johannesburg

Gingko
1 Dundalk Avenue, cnr Roscommon Avenue, Parkview, Johannesburg

Leafy Greens
Rocky Ridge Road, Muldersdrift, Johannesburg

The Greenside Café
34 Gleneagles Road, Greenside, Johannesburg

NATAL

Conscious Café
9 Renown Road, Westville, Durban

Earthmother Café
486 Lillian Ngoyi Road, Durban

Out to Lunch
28A Ronan Road, Durban

WESTERN CAPE

Ground Zero
122B Lower Main Road, Observatory, Cape Town

Lekker Vegan
37 Barrack Street, Shop 3, Cape Town

Maharajah Vegetarian
6 Rondebosch Court, Cape Town (at Fountain Square, Belmont Road, off Main Road)

Mig-21
Queens Road, Simon's Town

Nourish'd
177 Kloof Street, Gardens, Cape Town

Plant
8 Buiten Street, Cape Town

Pure Café
Grey Oak Centre, Unit 3, Main Road, Greyton

Pure Elixir Café
120 Bree Street, Cape Town;
127 Waterkant Street, Cape Town

Raw and Roxy
8 Bree Street, Cape Town CBD

Scheckter's Raw
98 Regent Street, Sea Point, Cape Town

The Hungry Herbivore
11 Orphan Street, Cape Town

MY FAVOURITE VEGAN-FRIENDLY RESTAURANTS

NATAL

Amaravathi Palki Restaurant
Suite 6, Tinsley House, 225 Musgrave Road, Berea, Durban

Chilliplum
Shop 9, Richden's Village Centre, Phase 2, 57 St Margarets Road, Hillcrest

Falafal Fundi
161 Gordon Road (at Florida Road), Durban

The Snooty Fox,
Fern Hills Hotel 3255, R103, Howick

WESTERN CAPE

Addis in Cape
41 Church Street, Cape Town CBD

Belmond Mount Nelson Hotel
76 Orange Street, Gardens, Cape Town

Beluga
Various locations

Craft Burger Bar
82 Regent Road, Sea Point,
Cape Town

Dolce Bakery
239C Lower Main Road, Observatory,
Cape Town

El Burro
81 Main Road, Green Point,
Cape Town

Enchanted Pizza and Pasta
4B, Cavalier Centre, 2 Parklands
Main Road, Parklands, Cape Town

Fat Cactus
Various locations, Cape Town

Ferdinando's Pizza
205 Lower Main Road, Observatory,
Cape Town

Greenhouse at Babylonstoren
Klapmuts-Simondium Road,
Simondium, near Cape Town

Green Leaf Café
Eversdal Road, Bellville, Cape Town

Harvest Café and Deli
102 Wale Street, Cape Town

Honest Chocolate
66 Wale St, Cape Town

Inside & You're Out (IYO Burgers)
Upstairs, 103 Bree St, Cape Town CBD

Jonkershuis
Groot Constantia wine estate, Groot
Constantia Road, Constantia, Cape
Town

Knead Bakery
Various locations, Cape Town

Lily's Restaurant
Shop 1, East-West Building, cor-
ner Beach Road and Surrey Place,
Mouille Point, Cape Town

Masala Dosa
167 Long Street, Cape Town

Massimo's
Oakhurst Farm Park, Main Road, Hout
Bay

Monocle & Mermaid
126 St Georges Street, Simon's Town,
Cape Town

Muse Fusion Food
152A Old Cape Road, Paradise,
Knysna

Newport Market and Deli
125 Beach Road, Mouille Point,
Cape Town

Peace of Eden
49 Rheenendal Road, Knysna

Royale Eatery
273 Long Street, Cape Town

Sababa
Shop 14, Piazza St John, 395 Main
Road, Sea Point, Cape Town

Saigon V
Corner Camp Street and Kloof Street,
Cape Town

Saucisse Deli
Unit A 112, Old Biscuit Mill, 375 Albert
Road, Woodstock, Cape Town

Sevruga
Shop 4, Quay 5, Victoria Wharf, V&A
Waterfront, Cape Town

Soet Bistro
11 Wellington Road, Durbanville,
Cape Town

The Courtyard Café
48 Main Road, Kalk Bay

The Dog's Bollocks at YARD
6 Roodehek Street, Gardens,
Cape Town

The Green Vine Eatery
Silvermist Wine Estate, Constantia
Main Road, Constantia, Cape Town

The Olive Tree
21 Main Street, Woodmill Lane
Shopping Centre, Knysna

The Strangers Club
1 Braemar Road, Green Point,
Cape Town

Unframed Ice Cream
45c Kloof Street, Gardens,
Cape Town

Warwick Wine Estate
R44, between Stellenbosch and
Klapmuts

Wild Sprout
Unit F, 179 Loop St, Cape Town CBD

Yindees
Corner Camp Street and Kloof Street,
Gardens, Cape Town

NATIONWIDE

ANAT

Col'Cacchio Pizzeria

Kauai

Mugg & Bean

Nino's

Nü Health Food Café

Ocean Basket

Osumo

Primi Piatti

RocoMamas

Simply Asia

Spur

Steers

Tasha's

Wellness Café

Wimpy

ACKNOWLEDGEMENTS

Thank you for having an open mind and heart as you browsed through the beautiful
pages of this book. I'm not here to convert you to my lifestyle of choice, but
I hope this book inspires your culinary creations and helps you see that
eating meals without eggs, dairy or meat can taste pretty darn good.
I can't thank NB Publishers enough for providing me with the incredible opportunity
of sharing my passion and helping to promote veganism in South Africa.
To all my friends — or should I say 'guinea pigs' — who have repeatedly tested
my recipes, thank you for your honest feedback and all the laughs around the
dinner table. Don, thank you for mentoring and motivating me from the moment
I pitched the idea to the day I submitted my final manuscript.
But my biggest gratitude goes to Crous, my brother and greatest fan, as well
as my parents, Leon and Elzette, who have shown me much support throughout this
journey: thank you for involving me in your love of cooking many years ago and
pushing me to proceed when my determination needed encouragement.
I am so grateful for the extra fridge you bought me to store my hundreds of attempts
in, for the ice buckets and plasters you had on hand when I cut and burnt my fingers,
for helping me wash pile upon pile of dirty dishes. Finally, thank you
for all the prayers, and the daily reminder that my strength comes from above.
Your unconditional love is in every bite of this book.

INDEX

Human & Rousseau

First published in 2018 by Human & Rousseau,
an imprint of NB Publishers, a division of Media24 Boeke (Pty) Ltd,
40 Heerengracht, Cape Town 8000

Publisher: Annake Müller
Editor: Tiara Walters
Proofreader: Glynne Newlands
Photographs: Myburgh du Plessis
Food preparation: Tani Kirsten
Food styling: Aletta Lintvelt
Cover and book design: Hanri Gerischer
Index: Anna Tanneberger

Reproduction by Resolution Colour (Pty) Ltd, Cape Town
Printed and bound in Malaysia by Times Offset

ISBN: 978-0-7981-7710-8

The information provided in this book is meant for educational and informational purposes only.
The knowledge and experience shared here are gained from personal experience. Should
professional assistance be needed, consult a qualified nutritionist or trained chef.